POLITICAL SCIENCE IN THEORY AND PRACTICE

POLITICAL SCIENCE IN THEORY AND PRACTICE

THE 'POLITICS' MODEL

Ruth Lane

Routledge
Taylor & Francis Group

LONDON AND NEW YORK

First published 1997 by M.E. Sharpe

Published 2015 by Routledge
2 Park Square, Milton Park, Abingdon, Oxon OX14 4RN
711 Third Avenue, New York, NY 10017, USA

Routledge is an imprint of the Taylor & Francis Group, an informa business

Library of Congress Cataloging-in-Publication Data

Lane, Ruth, 1935–
Political science in theory and practice : the
'politics' model / by Ruth Lane.
p.   cm.
Includes bibliographical references and index.
ISBN 1-56324-939-1 (cloth : alk. paper). —
ISBN 56324-940-5 (pbk. : alk. paper)
1. Political science.   I. Title.
JA71.L24   1996
320—dc20   96-21984
CIP

ISBN 13: 9781563249402 (pbk)
ISBN 13: 9781563249396 (hbk)

CONTENTS

PREFACE

A common reaction in the outside world to the admission that one is a political scientist, or is studying to be a political scientist, is the charge that political science is an oxymoron—or, more colloquially, the rude question "What's politics got to do with science?" followed by a skeptical roar of laughter. The public feeling seems to be that if political scientists were in possession of anything even faintly resembling a science, they could tell the world something beyond what is in the daily news, could provide not just the known facts but general explanations that would make the political world more understandable. This goal has been elusive. Even when sophisticated statistics are brought to bear on politics, the numbers frequently only repeat facts that were obvious enough to uninformed observers without going to all that statistical trouble. Something more has been needed.

This book argues that political science has over recent decades begun to fulfill its promise of providing in-depth explanations of political events from community politics to political parties to national development to international politics to all the nooks and crannies in which political interaction occurs. A kind of unobtrusive consensus has emerged among leading political scientists who have pursued their independent inquiries, following the natural contours of political life. These political scientists have not sought 'grand' theories, nor made great 'methodological' claims, but have directed their attention to real political problems where opportunities for gain and possibilities for trouble are inextricably mixed in daily political events. In doing what 'came naturally,' these political scientists have in effect created a working *model* of political behavior, a model that explains how individuals and groups, with varying resources and opportunities, engage in the political interactions that create, maintain, or destroy the political institutions, both formal and informal, under which all human beings must live. Using this model allows political scientists and other observers to get a better grip on political realities—the dark side and the light side, the conflict and the cooperation, the missed opportunities and the ill-taken roads—the whole fascinating system that we call politics.

This is not a 'proposed' model but one that has been worked out already by a panoply of well-known political scientists. The only step lacking to the completion of the model is to put a name on it, to call it the 'politics model' and in this way draw attention to the model's effectiveness in studying political events. The book takes this matter in several stages, first arguing that there is a recognizable kind of theory, concrete theory, that studies actual political interactions between real people and develops explanations for what happened and how; then moving to the full 'politics model' as it has been worked out over recent years (and past centuries) on a wide variety of political issues; and finally arguing that such a political model is in exact accord with the newest understanding of the philosophy of science, called scientific realism, which emphasizes just such process-oriented explanations. As part of this inquiry, I explore the various outcroppings of the politics model in comparative and American politics, in public administration, in international affairs; and inquire into the model's relationship with theories of the past, the far classical past as well as the early twentieth-century past.

The charm of the politics model is that it is practical, gives real answers, and enables real political observers to analyze the data that inundate all of us, in a way that has the potential to 'make sense' out of things. Theory has sometimes been touted as suitable only to the most refined intellects, to the most delicate spirits; but the politics model offers itself without pretension as a model willing to be of use to everyone. Those who love the political game as it is currently played will, through the politics model, learn to play the game better. Those who scorn everyday politics and seek to build kinder and gentler political systems will equally find the politics model useful, in telling them how to analyze their enemies and to encourage their faithful supporters. Even those who have no political agenda but only their deep curiosity about political affairs will find the politics model useful. It explains things and makes action thereby more effective.

Because the book is written in a tone that is clearly on the side of the politics model, I should probably state my relation to the matter. I grieve to say I did not invent the model, nor do I practice it in any major way. Rather, once upon a time I returned from an extended inquiry into the possibilities offered to political science by psychology, sociology, economics, and the various computer sciences and began to recognize that certain political scientists were doing better science than I had expected. Intrigued, I pursued them through various byways and found that in fact a large number of rather famous political scientists were working with the same inchoate model, lacking any appreciation that others were working in similar modes. I thought this to be a waste of a good idea, and I have tried in this book to explain their methods and their results as part of a unified model.

POLITICAL SCIENCE IN THEORY AND PRACTICE

1 INTRODUCTION TO THE POLITICS MODEL

Off with Their Heads!

Political science is one of the more difficult of the 'sciences' because political science is so severely hampered not only by the inherent difficulty of its subject matter but also by the hazards attached to the very tools with which it must work. Many times the political scientist closely resembles Lewis Carroll's Alice who, in Wonderland, was required to play croquet with a live flamingo for a mallet and a hedgehog for a ball, on a croquet ground that was all "ridges and furrows."

> The chief difficulty Alice found at first was in managing her flamingo: she succeeded in getting the body tucked away, comfortably enough, under her arm, with its legs hanging down, but generally, just as she had got its neck nicely straightened out, and was going to give the hedgehog a blow with its head, it would twist itself round and look up into her face with such a puzzled expression that she could not help bursting out laughing; and, when she had got its head down . . . again, it was very provoking to find that the hedgehog had unrolled itself, and was in the act of crawling away.

On top of her other problems, Alice was harassed by a Queen of Hearts who wandered about the croquet ground shouting "Off with her head!" While political scientists are perhaps less prone to laugh over their problems than was Alice (who was created by a mathematician), political scientists face problems comparable in nature and scope. The field upon which they play is bumpy and deceptive, their tools are inadequate to the task, and onlookers usually make complaints without regard to political scientists' success or failure.

This situation is naturally grievous to people who are fascinated by politics, impressed not only by the importance of the political policies that give shape to every part of human existence, but by the sheer excitement of the political spectacle—the wheeling and dealing, the battles and the strange bedfellows, the progress and the deadlocks, the triumphs and the disasters. This richness of subject matter has been a major barrier in political science research, however, because nothing ever seems to stand still long enough to be studied easily. Unlike physical scientists, political scientists have no quiet laboratories, no controlled experiments, no timeless truths. Political scientists, unlike, say, botanists, are a part of their topic. This unquestionably makes their enterprise more difficult.

Politics and Science

The hazards of studying politics have taken their toll on the political science discipline and its members, who have been prone not only to revolutions but occasionally to something resembling civil war. These divisions are not mitigated by the discipline's long and honorable tradition, dating back at least to Plato, because political scientists disagree, among other things, about when the discipline began and about its purpose as well. An important change came in the 1950s and 1960s with the 'behavioral revolution' that was to settle these issues and make political science *scientific*. This attempt at unity was not altogether successful, as it turned out, and many political scientists now believe that 1960 was the beginning of the problem rather than the solution.

Today there is an immense variety of possible 'approaches' to politics, but none that carries with it any measure of consensus; discussions of the field abound with terms such as tragedy, disenchantment, dead ends, and 'monsters' (Ricci 1984; Blalock 1984; Seidelman 1985; Gunnell 1986; Lindblom 1990; Lowi 1992; Roelofs 1994).[1] The situation seems anomalous in that so much effort has been devoted in the present century to the belief that political science was only a few easy steps away from being unified under new scientific approaches and techniques. At present the only consensus seems to be that nothing that has been tried has worked, and that nothing that might work has yet been tried.

In seeking to diagnose political science's ills, observers might notice that alone among the sciences, whether the 'soft' social sciences or the 'hard' physical ones, political science has never quite carved out its own specific identity. Sociology has 'fathers' such as Comte or Durkheim, who played major roles in defining the discipline; economics achieved definition even earlier, with Adam Smith. Political science, on the contrary, has either lacked paternity all together (a condition that in less tolerant times suggested illegitimacy), or it has had too many fathers, each passing along to his progeny contradictory lessons. The child caught between Plato and Machiavelli is very likely to have a neurotic adulthood.

Adding to the troubles of political science in recent years has been its position as a battleground between competing methodologies from other social sciences, especially economics and sociology. Sociologists diminished political science's sense of identity by arguing that political science was not a real field of study at all, but represented merely a partial aspect of the study of society in general and could be taken over quite nicely by sociology. On the other hand, economists have not bothered to argue the issues but have simply invaded political science, asserting that politics is just another form of economics and can be studied using the same techniques.[2]

By the early 1990s the battle between sociology and economics for the hearts and minds of political scientists reappeared in the form of state-in-society theories (Migdal 1988), which emphasized social system variables; and the new institutionalism (March and Olsen 1984) with its vigorous economic emphasis. Methodological issues as well were objects of discord. One major political scientist has described political scientists as comparable to 'solitary diners at a second-rate residential hotel,' each alone with his or her own definition of the field, 'uneasy' at their lonely 'separate tables' (Almond 1988, 828). Certainly this is a dismal commentary on the state of any discipline.[3]

A Politics Model

Like Mark Twain's death (the reports of which, he said, had been greatly exaggerated), the disarray of the political science discipline may not be as desperate as it sometimes appears. There is another interpretation of political science that is much more hopeful, if iconoclastic. This interpretation argues that underneath the stylish diversity of the discipline there is a more enduring tradition, one that has never announced itself with bells and whistles but has proceeded in its own terms and along its own paths.

This alternative interpretation, which is the subject of the present study, highlights a variety of works in American politics, comparative politics, international relations, and public administration that are by well-known political scientists but have never been thought of as comprising a definable approach to political science. Yet because the works are recognized as landmarks in political research, and because analysis shows their underlying methods to be so similar, it seems appropriate for political science to acknowledge the approach.

These works in political research and theory represent a hidden tradition, a tradition that is essentially political (rather than sociological, economic, historical, or psychological), and one that seems to emerge in many sectors of the field when political scientists 'do' political science rather than engaging in grand debates or in esoteric methodologies. A convenient term for this approach is the 'politics model.'

The name is appropriate because the analytic approach used in this type of research centers itself upon the kind of politics often compared, in the ancient joke, to sausage, where if one wishes to enjoy the result, one is well advised not to watch it being made. Political scientists have tended to denigrate this 'sausage' politics, but the politics model affirms it as the very essence of the political process.

The model is political in a higher sense also, for it is founded not on human subservience to social, economic, or governmental institutions, but instead emphasizes the power of strategically situated individuals to understand, confront, and change circumstances.

Two questions are central in introducing the politics model: Who practices it, and what do they do? First the question of who practices it. A representative if incomplete list would include:[4]

In the field of American politics,

- Nelson Polsby (1983) on party change,
- Jacobson and Kernell (1983) on congressional elections,
- Miller and Jennings (1986) on presidential party conventions,
- Stephen Skowronek (1982) on U.S. national development and (1984) on presidential decision making;

in the field of comparative politics,

- Samuel Huntington (1968) on institutional politics,
- Robert Bates (1981) on African agriculture,

- Przeworski and Sprague (1986) on electoral socialism,
- Robert Dahl (1966) on political oppositions,
- North and Thomas (1973) on political-economic development,
- Barrington Moore (1966) on transitions to modernity,
- Joel Migdal (1988) on the creation of the state;

in the field of international relations,

- George and Smoke (1974) on international deterrence theory,
- Richard Rosecrance (1963) on international organization,
- Stephen D. Krasner (1983) on international regimes;

in the field of public administration and policy,

- Aaron Wildavsky (Pressman and Wildavsky 1979) on implementation,
- Terry Moe (1980) on interest-group organization and politics,
- Elinor Ostrom (Kiser and Ostrom 1982) on institutional rule structures, and
- Norton Long (1962) on community politics.

This seems, undoubtedly, a very mixed bag of political scientists, all to be 'doing the same thing.' Can any single method be characteristic of so diverse a collection of political scientists? This brings us to the second question: What is it that they do, in using the politics model as the basis of their analysis?

Defining the Politics Model

On the surface, the method that these political scientists practice does not seem particularly marvelous; this modesty of the approach is exactly why it has not hitherto been recognized as a distinct method. The starting point of the method is to focus on political events in their rich complexity, and then carefully to take these political events apart, into their individual components and sequences. Analysts then seek to determine how these individual components interact, connected by a sort of behavioral 'logic,' to produce particular political outcomes. In short, they build a 'model.'

A model in political science is approximately what it is in everyday discourse: a simplified, usually reduced version of the real world. A model train lacks size, lacks real diesel or steam engines, lacks passengers, conductors, or engineers; but the essential ideas are present—the locomotive, passenger cars, caboose, tracks. And most important, it moves over the tracks, over bridges, from station to station or point to point 'just like a real train.' Models in science are similar: They include the essential elements of the process in question and show how these elements are interconnected to produce the results characteristic of the thing being modeled (Lave and March 1975).

Let us try to be more systematic about the characteristics of the politics model. Ten points of emphasis define it.

1. The politics model begins from an interest in full-blown political events such as campaigns, wars, reform movements, relations between legislatures and executives, policy development and implementation, and so on. It does not merely abstract single variables for study but widens its lens to encompass whole sequences, whole multilevel interactive situations.

2. The politics model focuses on individual decision makers as the basic elements of analysis. If any conclusions are drawn at the level of the whole political system, they are the result of individual interactions, not the needs or desires or indeed the good of the whole system. This is why the term "concrete" is used of the model.

3. Analysis of the cognitive structures of the participants is made a separate, important analytic step in the politics model. Attention is put not on how the observer sees the matter, but on how the participants themselves define the situation and the issues of which they are a part. This does not involve 'deep' studies of subjectivity, but only a recognition that the participants' views need to be considered, rather than allowing the scientist to define things in his or her own way.

4. Separate but related is the politics model's emphasis on the explicit study of what goals the participants are pursuing, allowing for a wide range of possible purposes, including the social, the ethical, even the spiritual, in addition to the economic and the political.

5. The politics model is centrally defined by its attention to the structures of interaction among individuals as crucial to determining the actual outcomes of the political process. No person's individual act creates a specific outcome; outcomes depend not only on what individuals do but on how other individuals act and react to them.

6. Individuals must be described fully, in the politics model, in terms of the resources they bring to the fray. Some are rich, powerful, and clever; some are poor, weak, and foolish. Or people may be rich and foolish. The types of resources, and their particular combinations, are decisive in creating opportunities, necessities, and possibilities for the different participants.

7. Norms, customs, rules, and institutions are of central importance for the politics model. Sometimes rules involve specific decisions about distribution—who gets what parts of the buffalo that has just been killed. More important are the longer-term rules that define, for the group in question, rights and duties and the meaning of 'justice' for the society.

8. 'Politics,' according to the model, involves the multifaceted negotiations over these rules and institutions that distribute resources, rights, and honors. Particular conflicts are interesting because they settle the various issues of distribution that occur in the course of the week. More interesting, however, are the long-term arrangements made by the society, the rules about who is entitled to what, and who has the authority to make, maintain, or change the rules. These rules may sometimes be 'fair' to all in the society, but in most cases (both in democracies and nondemocracies) the rules are slanted to favor certain groups over others. These rules are the 'constitution' of society; to control these rules is the aim of the participants.

9. The politics model is characterized also by formal qualities, by the shape in which it organizes its elements, by the logic with which it connects its ideas and explanations. This dynamic logic is sequential and chronological; showing how people's choices at one moment in time change the context of interaction, so that the choices of the same or other people at subsequent times are influenced.

10. Finally, the politics model is built on the premise that science must go *beyond* mere empiricism, beyond simply studying the surface of events, and must dig beneath the appearances to the deeper explanations that can be found in the underlying processes that make up the restless variety of behavior that is typically designated as 'politics.' Where older scientific methods sought universality by rising above reality to grand (and sometimes empty) abstractions, the politics model works in a different way. Instead of mapping surfaces, the politics model strips away surfaces and finds universal processes at the heart of events. While historical differences will mark these pro-

cesses, the processes themselves are universal—they are what everyone calls 'politics.'

The politics model defines politics as the strategic interaction of persons and other actors, who have different beliefs, attitudes, values, and goals as they decide particular conflicts over the distribution of resources and general issues of political rules within a context of norms, expectations, and institutions. Any of the rules, expectations, and institutions may be revised, maintained, or inverted by the individuals who win the right to control them, in the course of those political negotiations that are sometimes called cooperation, and sometimes are called war, and are usually somewhere between the two. As Eulau graphically expresses this definition of politics, it is

> . . . ruling and obeying, persuading and resisting, promising and disappointing, coercing and freeing, compromising and claiming, deceiving and unmasking, negotiating and bargaining, neglecting and representing, fearing and fighting . . . tendencies-in-tension, often opposed but also attracting each other. . . . (Eulau 1986, 1)

The Affirmation of Politics

To the ancient question of what is the distinctive quality of the events studied by political science, the politics model returns the delphic response—'politics.' By politics it means raw politics, the kind we, as persons of good will, often remark upon with scorn. "If anyone had the public interest at heart, this program would have prospered, but it was killed by 'politics.'" Translated, this means often that selfish people with selfish agendas used their official positions and resources to protect their own skins or their own turf. We may prefer to turn our backs on such mendacity, but the politics model pounces on it.

Those who use the politics model explicitly bring into their purview just those behaviors that other political scientists often deliberately leave out. The politics model includes actors who may be rational sometimes, or who may be adaptive sometimes, or at other times may be 'culturally' rational. But the politics model includes actors who play politics in an old-fashioned way that the other social sciences leave out when describing human behavior.

Schelling (1963) has argued that human interactions, from family to church to nation-state to bowling club, all contain the possibility of war by some means or another. The politics model affirms this constant potential for conflict as its basis and is thereby able, while matching the microanalycity of economics and sociology, to provide a quintessentially political model. The politics model is thus in harmony with developments in other social sciences, but stands distinctively on its own political ground.

A Process Model of Party Reform

A sketch of a study of party reform, discussed in more detail in Chapter 3, will make the 'politics' approach clearer. Say a political party is taken over by a new group of members, who set about changing the rules to benefit persons they feel have been inadequately represented in the past. New criteria are established that grass-roots politicians must follow, but the uncertainty about just what will be 'acceptable' causes the local politicians to puzzle over what method they must use to choose candidates. In America at least, 'democracy' is always acceptable, and so there is adoption of mass democracy rules for candidate elections.

Given that choices on candidates are no longer made solely by party regulars but by the electorate, new types of candidates enter campaigns, and they use different types of campaign strategies. When they win office, they govern in ways different from past officeholders and are considered less competent than earlier officials (Polsby 1983). The pattern is one where individual actions at one time change the expectations of other individuals at another time, and the new expectations change behaviors, which in turn change the expectations for a further group. Thus process models are based on individual actions, but these actions are interactions that combine into dynamic systems.

Is the Proof in the Pudding?

Has the politics model earned legitimacy by any discoveries made by those who practice it? The record is not at all bad. Long-term observers of political science will recall a variety of instances in which certain scholars, collected here as practitioners of the politics model, have dealt with a variety of political events and problems in ways that, in retrospect, turned out to be more satisfactory to the discipline than were the 'fancier' methodological studies.

• In an era when most students of comparative politics thought that economic and political development was an easy, smooth, and surely successful effort by the Third World, Huntington's (1968) politics model showed that nations could stall, go backward, or fail entirely as politicians fought over the right to rule.

• When 'community power' theorists argued at an abstract level over questions of local governance by powerful elites, Long (1962) found that most leaders never even attended the meetings at which they were supposed to conspire together over issues of governance and power.

• In the face of enduring international traditions that treated nation-states as unified wholes, Rosecrance (1963) dug into the domestic sources of international behavior, and the larger effects they imposed upon the international system of Europe.

• A long-running debate over whether 'economics' determines the outcomes of congressional elections, or, as surveys indicated, citizens 'vote for the best candidate' was reconciled by Jacobson and Kernell's (1983) showing that certain economic conditions brought out certain types of candidates, so that both views were partially correct.

• The assumption that in a democracy, interest groups are a sort of automatic reflection of underlying voter interests was challenged by Moe's (1980) politics model showing how the emergence of interest groups depended on the activities of entrepreneurs who worked within miniature political systems in the effort to create, maintain, and fight off challenges to their leadership.

• In a time of enthusiasm for reform in American politics, Polsby (1983) showed that reformers often fail to foresee the long-term effects of their well-intentioned changes.

• The usually polemical issue of 'why socialism fails' was treated elegantly by Przeworski and Sprague's (1986) model showing that under certain economic conditions socialists' opportunities are inherently contradictory.

• Bookshelves full of optimistic hopes for change in the underdeveloped nations were put in question by arguments (Bates 1981;

Migdal 1988) that political leaders are not and cannot be interested solely in the 'good of the nation' but must first contrive to stay in office.

Overall, therefore, the record of the politics model in practice has been a notable one. Unexamined assumptions have been laid bare by political scientists using the politics model. Unrealistic hopes have been punctured. Artificial contradictions have been cleared away. But the politics model has not been merely iconoclastic. It has over the years explored and illuminated a variety of important political questions:

- the nature of democracy, fascism, and other forms of states;
- the causes of war and peace;
- why popular programs may completely fail;
- how states organize themselves into international systems;
- the nature of democratic reform;
- the origins of peasants' behavior;
- the nature of the rule systems that guide political actions;
- why some nations achieve stability and economic development;
- and why some do not;
- how U.S. presidents and presidential candidates attract campaign workers;
- the politics of interest groups;
- the effect of economic conditions on political choices;
- why things usually go wrong, and why some things sometimes go right.

To show in more detail how these topics have been approached, analyzed, and evaluated through the politics model is the subject of succeeding chapters.

Comparisons with Other Social Models

The essential elements of the 'politics' model are similar in some ways to other social science models, but are in other ways markedly different. For instance, the politics model, like other well-known social models, is based on the actions of individuals or small groups. But the politics model includes a variety of contextual factors that are usually missing from other models.[5]

First among these important political factors are the specific resources held by the individual participants. Politics is not a market in which all are equal but a more or less overt struggle in which some have more wealth, status, or power than others and try to use it to dominate others; and where the others may try to deprive them of that wealth, status, or power. In short, there is inequality, domination, conflict, and, in some cases, war.

A second important difference between the politics model and other social models is that the actors in politics are everywhere constrained in their behavior by the presence of norms, cultures, rules, and institutions. Such norms and rules are actually another kind of resource, because they give some persons rights over others, and distribute benefits and disabilities in various ways among the people under their jurisdiction. Since all political individuals are assumed to be goal-directed, they may find that the distribution of goods as defined by the status quo is not satisfactory to them. This leads to the interactive nexus we know as 'politics,' where people with different goals work with, for, and against each other to change or maintain the principles by which their political systems operate.

Recognition of research based on the politics model contains elements that suggest a more creative relationship between political science and the other social sciences. In the past, political science has seemed least among equals, forced to borrow theory from economics (Downs 1957; Buchanan and Tullock 1965), from sociology (Almond and Coleman 1960), or psychology (Lasswell 1945). Indeed, since the inception of modern social science, political science has often been embattled, struggling to hold on to some portion of the field that could be called distinctly its own against competitors who claimed politics was secondary and must give way to their greater primacy in explaining human behavior.

But by using models adapted from elsewhere, political science often had to behave like Procrustes, cutting off heads and feet so that political persons could be fitted to social or economic beds. The politics model restructures the relationship between politics and the other social sciences by bringing to political science a model of behavior that is unique to its own particular data and concerns, but is as potentially rigorous as economic and social psychological models.

The other social sciences have made their progress toward scientific rigor by finding their 'basic unit' and building theory upon that unit with rigorous logical methods. Economics has employed as its basic unit the concept of economic man, who is postulated to make decisions on the basis of self-interest, maximization, and rationality. Social psychology has similarly focused on adaptive decision makers who in the circumstances presented by real events choose the course of action that in the past proved most satisfactory (both models are beautifully described in Lave and March 1975). These approaches have often seemed to reduce politics to more basic decision processes, arguing in effect that there was nothing distinctive about political behavior, nothing that could not be subsumed under economic or social perspectives. The politics model suggests a path out of this dilemma by presenting a simple rigorous model that is recognizably political.

A Different Philosophy of Science

Anyone who claims that political science has an 'unnoticed' tradition of research, a tradition dating back at least to the 1930s and capable of providing a unifying thread to the discipline, must expect to be presented with the question "How does it come about that nobody noticed it before?" The question is entirely natural and deserves a convincing answer. Unfortunately, the answer is not as short as one might wish, and Chapter 6 is devoted to the issues. But a preliminary answer is appropriate here. It involves the definition of science.

The definition of science is important because it determines, at a given time and place, what kinds of research are legitimate. If 'science' involves curing disease through incantations to the gods, someone trying to introduce penicillin may be seen as an agent of the devil and driven out. If 'science' is defined as neoclassical economics, someone trying to introduce convex indifference curves and nonequilibrium solutions may find an equally unkind audience (Waldrop 1992).

Science, as Thomas Kuhn (1962) has famously taught, is in this sense political: It proceeds by 'revolutions' from one paradigm to another, and what is accepted as reality in one paradigm will differ from that which is accepted as reality in another. The problem with recognition of the politics model has been that it did not fit the definition of science popular in the political science discipline.

The politics model is scientific but in a new way. In order to get the flavor of the difference a new scientific approach makes, in respect to research, it must be considered against a background of the 'positivist' philosophy of science that guided political science during its earlier behavioral period.[6] Positivism defined science in terms of universal statements about the relationship between small sets of abstract variables, and it emphasized the empirical testing of such operationally defined hypotheses in order to falsify those that were not supported by the data. Its principles are summarized by Holt and Turner (1970) in the following terms:

> Ideally, scientific research in its simplest form involves, first, the deduction of a hypothesis from a set of theoretical propositions, and, second, investigations to determine whether the facts of relationships predicted by the hypothesis manifest themselves empirically. Typically, the hypothesis involves a predicted relationship between at least two variables and takes the general form of "If A, then B." (p. 6)

This approach came into full bloom in political science in the 1960s, when behavioralist works such as *The American Voter* (Campbell, Converse, Miller, and Stokes 1964) and *The Civic Culture* (Almond and Verba 1963) overturned old views of the democratic citizen and the participatory American, and plunged political science into the universal search for economic and sociological explanations of political behavior. As time went on, 'scientific' political science came to involve the collection and statistical analysis of vast archives of empirical data. Research that did not fit this model was not 'real' research, although it might be admitted as useful groundwork. Any political scientist who delved too deeply into history, political institutions, or specific political cases was generally considered to be outside the methodological mainstream of the discipline.

The New Philosophy of Science

This situation appeared to have no solution under the positivist aegis. Political science seemed to be doing what it had been taught, and yet many different voices were raised in complaint (Ricci 1984; Seidelman 1985; Gunnell 1986; Lowi 1992).

The 'solution' came, in some sense, from both within and without the discipline. Within political science, the unobtrusive tradition I have called the politics model went its cheerful way, investigating political phenomena in all sorts of areas and finding interesting results that could be neither ignored nor classified—the research simply did not fit in the existing categories.[7]

On the other hand, philosophers of science soon turned away from positivism and developed their scientific theories in new directions. These philosophers of science basically argued that no one, even physicists, had ever done science in the manner defined by positivism; and by the 1990s the philosophers had defined an alternative, 'scientific realism,' that formed a new orthodoxy. This new philosophy of science provided a new definition of science, and the 'unclassifiable' political scientists who practiced the politics model fell straight into it.

Scientific realism, developed by philosophers trained in physics and other 'hard' sciences, puts its primary emphasis on *explanation* of physical processes as a function of close causal analysis into underlying patterns of interaction. Where positivists were concerned solely to map empirical correlations on the surface of things, scientific realists plunge into the depths, seeking ever deeper levels of explanation (Giere 1988; Churchland and Hooker 1985; Hilton 1988).

Such an approach, transported into political science, would mandate the kinds of analysis characterized in the present work as concrete theory or the politics model. Analysts have not simply recorded abstract correlations, but have gone beneath the surface to investigate the underlying mechanisms. The approach taken to analyzing these mechanisms is that of model building. Rather than a multivariate correlation of variables, concrete theorists have used the scientific realist approach of defining process-oriented models of how things happen in various political settings (Suppe 1989; Pitt 1988).

Essential to this view of science is the historical dimension: that events at one point in time influence events later in time, usually because past events are turned into new expectations, norms, or institutions, within which behavior must proceed at the next step. The form of scientific realist explanation is not a simple linear correlation, therefore, but a model of process.

In such a political process model, the individual actors (however many there may be) cooperate, compete, go to war, or refuse to go to war, and the interactions have some determinate outcome. Resources are retained or redistributed, there are winners or losers, rules are maintained or modified, and all these results affect subsequent interactions. This sort of a model is tested not by statistical correlations but by its coincidence with observable facts.

The spirit of the scientific realist approach is vividly defined by one of its major proponents, Rom Harre. The topic is an eighteenth-century planetarium.

> At Eindhoven, a gentleman amused himself by cutting circular slits in the ceiling of an upper room of his house, through which rods were suspended and on the end of which hung the planets. The whole was, and indeed is, exquisitely painted in blue and gold. A wait of an hour or so enables one to detect a little movement in the inner planets. . . . Were we, the spectators of the show, to leave it with a few notes of the regularities observed, like modern Babylonians? Not at all. . . . For an additional guilder a ladder was revealed in a cupboard, and up we went . . . there was a fantastic contrivance of wooden gears, huge wheels and enormous weights, from the behavior of which the regularities in the movements of the dependent planets flowed. (Harre 1970, 27)

This manner of penetrating behind the surface to the processes that may be hidden but are the causal root of appearances is exactly the approach taken by all of those who utilize the politics model discussed here. They have paid their guilder and gotten a look at the hidden 'mechanics' of the political process.

Different Levels of the Political Inquiry

The approach defined here comes at three conceptually distinct levels: It encompasses a type of theory, a method, and a metaphysic. When it is theory, I have called it 'concrete' theory (Chapter 2); and, as a method, the 'politics' model (Chapter 3). At the level of philosophies of science, concrete theory and the politics model break from the old positivist canon and illustrate a new metaphysic, that of 'scientific realism' (Chapter 6).

As a body of theory, the politics model has guided inquiry into a wide variety of questions and issues in political science. I have called this type of theory 'concrete' theory to emphasize its difference from many other forms of theory that do not keep so close to the nuts-and-bolts aspects of political realities (Lane 1990). Studies at the theoretical level include voting in congressional elections (Jacobson and Kernell 1983), agricultural problems in Africa (Bates 1981), elite electoral strategies (Przeworski and Sprague 1986), national economic development in Europe (North and Thomas 1973), presidential leadership (Skowronek

1984), presidential campaigns (Miller and Jennings 1986), the hazards of policy implementation (Pressman and Wildavsky 1979), and international deterrence strategies (George and Smoke 1974).

What serves to unify these diverse research areas in the present case is their use of a common method. Method, as distinguished from theory or metaphysic, involves "mid-range techniques and principles" that are "sufficiently general to be common to all sciences, or to a significant part of them" (Kaplan 1964, 23). The 'politics model' summarizes for political science such a set of principles common to works of the sort mentioned above. Like, say, the economic model, the politics model does not specify particular hypotheses, theories, or conclusions, but provides axioms, approaches, and rules of analysis that guide researchers who are engaged in empirical studies. As 'method,' the politics model includes the following general propositions:

1. The analytic axiom, which holds that the best route to understanding complex phenomena is to break them into their component parts, usually individuals, sometimes groups acting in concert.

2. The axiom of connectedness, which holds that the parts must be understood in relation to one another and to the whole system they constitute; in the politics model this whole includes institutions, both formal and informal.

3. The process axiom, which focuses attention on the specific interactions among the individuals and groups involved in the analysis, and which defines process as decisive in determining outcomes; these outcomes, in addition, may affect institutions.

4. The politics axiom, which accepts as central to interaction the type of conflict behavior not always included in sociological models, where there is at least the preference for unity, or in economic models, where there is usually the hope of mutual benefit. Conflict behavior— 'politics'—may include persuasion, influence, coercion, deception, threats, strategies, tactics, and various degrees of actual force. The outcomes may entail exploitation or destruction of the losers.

While the *topic* of research may vary, therefore, the *method* remains constant. Where the topics of research are relatively narrow, it is appropriate to talk about concrete theory or theories. Where the subject itself broadens to focus on the whole political process, the term politics 'model' better captures the exercise. Chapter 3 analyzes the use of this broader politics model by a range of political scientists:

Barrington Moore's (1966) study of national development;
Norton Long's (1958) inquiry into urban administration;
Stephen Skowronek's (1982) analysis of U.S. political history;
Robert Dahl's (1966) evaluation of political oppositions;
Joel Migdal's (1988) essay on strategies of political survival;
Richard Rosecrance's (1966) work in grounded international theory;
Terry Moe's (1980) political theory of organizational behavior;
Samuel Huntington's (1968) analysis of political change and decay;
Nelson Polsby's (1983) evaluation of American party reform.

Finally, at the third level of analysis, it must be noted that models and theories do not exist in a vacuum, but are located within some overarching sets of scientific principles (a metaphysic) that give them shape and meaning. The nature of reality would be a subject of little interest to anyone but pure philosophers were it not that scientific theories acquire their legitimacy and their justification from the precepts laid down by these metaphysical systems. A scientific model will be acceptable or unacceptable not in absolute terms but in terms of the metaphysic by which it is judged.

In understanding the politics model, therefore, the nature of the new metaphysic of 'scientific realism' is important, because it defines what now constitutes the rules by which scientific work will be evaluated. Because of the importance of this issue, it must be discussed in some detail in order to properly evaluate the status of concrete theory and the politics model; but because of difficulty of the issue, it is left until Chapter 6, when the definition and operation of the politics model have been laid out more fully.[8]

A Field Guide to Theory Watching

The politics model is sometimes difficult to recognize because most of its practitioners do not loudly announce their methodological purposes; many writers are themselves not fully aware of the methodological stature of their research.

Very often readers come upon concrete theory inadvertently, taking up a book on a topic in which they are interested and finding as they read deeper that they have gotten more than they bargained for. Instead of a descriptive history, replete with human-interest anecdotes to motivate the reader's attention, a certain logic begins to manifest itself in the presentation. Willingly or not, the reader is taken on an analysis of the facts that is so firm, so disciplined, so probing, so vigorous, that the swift discursive flow is slowed or halted. The text becomes dense; ideas, propositions, hypotheses (often disguised as highly opinionated discourse), follow in rapid succession and in what may seem a tendentious arrangement.

Seeing these signs the reader must shift gears, out of the relaxed overdrive with which one absorbs interesting facts and into a more rugged gear designed for hills and harsh terrain. Analysis based on the politics model may annoy the reader's sensibilities with its rigor. Even where there exists a predisposition to agree with the concrete theorist's facts or conclusions, the density of the text offers many occasions to object, to disagree, to protest. If one has characterized the work in hand as one of description, one is apt to feel betrayed by what seems to be excessive interpretation. Only by recategorizing the effort as a theoretic one does the reader become sensible of its power.

The Practice of Political Research

The challenges raised by social and political issues are as pressing in the late twentieth century as they have ever been. More than ever before, the scientific and technological resources to provide the world's population with a better life seem available. That this promise often is not fulfilled is clearly a result of human beings' inability to understand themselves and the societies they have created and within which they must live.

The politics model, as it is described in the present work, does not by any means solve such large issues, but it does take a firm direction toward self-understanding in immediate things. Why a policy, though popular, may nonetheless fail, is not unrelated to why societies fail. The attractive characteristic of the politics model, for those who are ambitious for social theory, is that while each of the scientists starts on different practical problems, their findings tend to converge. This suggests that useful, unified social theory may not be impossible. It is a hope worth exploring with an open mind.

The politics model has been developed for the most part independently of these concerns, but it speaks directly to the issues they raise. Where political science has frequently rejected 'politics' in favor of higher purposes or programs, the politics model centers directly upon the political process with all its frequently unsavory aspects. The politics model may seem a bit common, compared with following Plato to the edge of the world and looking off at the view. Nonetheless it has proved a useful citizen and deserves more attention than it has received.

The Structure of the Book

The argument of the present work begins in Chapter 2 with the 'first stage' of discovery of the politics model, which centers on a type of theory originally called 'concrete,' directed to the construction of process-oriented explanations of specific political problems and issues—how voters decide in congressional elections, why socialism fails so frequently, the foundations of international conflict, and so on.

Chapter 3 develops the full-scale thesis of the book, that concrete forms of theory may take on such wide-ranging political issues, and may use methods so coherent, that a model emerges that is equivalent to the best models of other social sciences but is distinctively political. The model focuses so directly on concrete political processes that it is natural to call it the 'politics model.' Examples are given from all four subfields of the political science discipline, and analysis is directed to making clear the theoretical quality of methods that very often are not recognized as qualifying as theoretical.

The remaining three chapters may be read in any order. Those who are familiar with the political science discipline, and who are distrustful of the thesis that a politics model exists, may wish to skip to Chapter 6, which goes into current discourse in the philosophy of science in order to show that the model fits the newest scientific metaphysic. Chapter 6 also shows how the new philosophy of science, within which the politics model is contained, differs from the older metaphysic of positivism.

Chapter 4 takes up three issues relevant to the politics model. First, it suggests some examples from the distant past and more recent past of the ways earlier theorists have employed the model. Second, the chapter shows how the politics model can be used to give coherence and scientific import to studies that appear to be historical or anthropological. Finally, in order to show that not all good political writing can be defined within the rubric of the politics model, the chapter discusses two works, one wholly empirical, the other highly conceptual, which must be distinguished from the politics model.

Chapter 5 expands the analysis to a specific case of theory building in political science—structural functionalism—and shows that the political scientists who tried to utilize this very abstract approach were able to do so only sporadically and that when they wanted to make meaningful generalizations about the process of political development, they actually turned to a model identical to that which is here called the politics model. This discussion tends to support the idea that the politics model is widespread, and if acknowledged by the field can serve a useful research role.

Notes

1. Roelofs (1994, 264) proclaims the 'dead end' of the Bentley tradition, and seeks a return to theoretical concerns (1994, 264); Lindblom (1990, 194) denounces social science and political science as frivolous and careless and says they must use more flexible and effective methods; Lowi (1992, 5) claims political science has become "dismal" and has removed itself "two or three levels away from sensory experience." Elster (1989, 3–10) complains of the weaknesses of positivism and says deeper explanation, based on underlying causal mechanisms, is needed; Blalock (1984, 10) argues that the social sciences have created a shapeless monster instead of a discipline, and that they must seek some kind of consensus in the place of their present fragmentation; Gunnell (1986, 41) sees an estrangement between research and actual politics and urges a search for natural laws of underlying processes. While disagreement is normal within scientific disciplines, the condition of political science appears in all this to have well exceeded the normal bounds.

2. The idea of defining political science as a distinct discipline because it alone studied governmental institutions was an old solution to the problem of definition, but it was easy to see, even before the behavioralists made the point, that government was only a minor part of the political system as a whole. Parsons's dismissal of political science as a discipline was based on his belief that it was not built on analytical theory, unlike economics, and lacked a conceptual structure of its own; political science was thus merely "synthetic" (Parsons 1951, 126–27). Aristotle said the same thing, but he called political science the 'master' science. But at that time in history, political scientists gave Parsons more attention than Aristotle.

3. An apparently more positive view of the discipline is found in the two excellent volumes edited by Finifter (1983, 1993) for the American Political Science Association. The volumes' purpose is to provide current summaries and evaluations of the several fields and subfields within the discipline, and they fulfill this purpose to an admirable degree. Close reading, however, reveals that many of the authors are highly critical of the fields they present, and a comparison of the two volumes suggests lack of scholarly continuity in many areas of inquiry.

4. I have restricted the examples to major political scientists on the grounds that their works will be the most familiar, and their use of the approach the most convincing. The politics model can also be found, however, in many other works. The means of identifying it are discussed later in the chapter.

5. The best starting point for an analysis of modeling is Lave and March (1975). Downs (1957) is still the classic example of the creative power of models in political analysis.

6. Political scientists can ignore the full history of positivism, which began in the 1920s in Vienna (Ayer 1959), and can concentrate instead upon its arrival in political science in the years after the Second World War, when a whole generation of political scientists decided that their history should be discarded and that a general effort should be made to turn the discipline into something truly 'scientific'; the spokesman for this "behavioral" movement initially was David Easton (1953).

7. Many who used the politics model were at pains to separate their own work from that of others in their field, but they had no ready label with which to identify their work. See, for instance, Migdal (1988), George and Smoke (1974).

8. The degree of difference within political science on these methodological issues is clearly demonstrated in the sharp reaction to the very modest methodological suggestions contained in a recent work on qualitative research (see Laitin, Caporaso, Collier, Rogowski, and Tarrow 1995).

References

Almond, Gabriel A. 1988. "Separate Tables: Schools and Sects in Political Science." *PS: Political Science and Politics* 21, no. 4 (fall): 828–42.

Almond, Gabriel A., and James S. Coleman, eds. 1960. *The Politics of the Developing Areas*. Princeton, NJ: Princeton University Press.

Almond, Gabriel A., and Sidney Verba. 1963. *The Civic Culture*. Princeton, NJ: Princeton University Press.

Ayer, A. J., ed. 1959. *Logical Positivism*. New York: The Free Press.

Bates, Robert H. 1981. *Markets and States in Tropical Africa: The Political Basis of Agricultural Policies*. Berkeley: University of California Press.

Blalock, Hubert H., Jr. 1984. *Basic Dilemmas in the Social Sciences*. Beverly Hills, CA: Sage Publications.

Buchanan, James M., and Gordon Tullock. 1965. *The Calculus of Consent (1963)*. Ann Arbor: University of Michigan Press.

Campbell, Angus, Philip E. Converse, Warren E. Miller, and Donald E. Stokes. 1964. *The American Voter*. New York: John Wiley and Sons.

Carroll, Lewis. 1960. *Alice's Adventures in Wonderland* (1865) and *Through the Looking Glass* (1871). New York: Signet.

Churchland, Paul M., and Clifford A. Hooker, eds. 1985. *Images of Science: Essays on Realism and Empiricism with a Reply from Bas C. Van Fraassen*. Chicago: University of Chicago Press.

Dahl, Robert A., ed. 1966. *Political Oppositions in Western Democracies*. New Haven, CT: Yale University Press.

Downs, Anthony. 1957. *An Economic Theory of Democracy*. New York: Harper and Row.

Easton, David. [1953] 1964. *The Political System: An Inquiry into the State of Political Science*. Chicago: University of Chicago Press.

Elster, Jon. 1989. *Nuts and Bolts for the Social Sciences*. Cambridge: Cambridge University Press.

Eulau, Heinz. 1986. *Politics, Self, and Society: A Theme and Variations.* Cambridge, MA: Harvard University Press.

Finifter, Ada W., ed. 1983. *Political Science: The State of the Discipline.* Washington, DC: American Political Science Association.

———. 1993. *Political Science: The State of the Discipline II.* Washington, DC: American Political Science Association.

George, Alexander, and Richard Smoke. 1974. *Deterrence in American Foreign Policy: Theory and Practice.* New York: Columbia University Press.

Giere, Ronald N. 1988. *Explaining Science: A Cognitive Approach.* Chicago: University of Chicago Press.

Gunnell, John G. 1986. *Between Philosophy and Politics: The Alienation of Political Theory.* Amherst: University of Massachusetts Press.

Harre, Romano. 1986. *Varieties of Realism: A Rationale for the Natural Sciences.* New York: Basil Blackwell.

Hilton, Denis J., ed. 1988. *Contemporary Science and Natural Explanation: Commonsense Conceptions of Causality.* New York: New York University Press.

Holt, Robert T., and John E. Turner, eds. 1970. *The Methodology of Comparative Research.* New York: The Free Press.

Huntington, Samuel P. 1968. *Political Order in Changing Societies.* New Haven, CT: Yale University Press.

Jacobson, Gary C., and Samuel Kernell. 1983. *Strategy and Choice in Congressional Elections.* 2d ed. New Haven, CT: Yale University Press.

Kaplan, Abraham. 1964. *The Conduct of Inquiry.* San Francisco: Chandler.

Kiser, Larry L., and Elinor Ostrom. 1982. "A Metatheoretical Synthesis of Institutional Approaches." In *Strategies of Political Inquiry,* ed. Elinor Ostrom, pp. 179–222. Beverly Hills, CA: Sage Publications.

Krasner, Stephen D., ed. 1983. *International Regimes.* Ithaca, NY: Cornell University Press.

Kuhn, Thomas S. 1962. *The Structure of Scientific Revolutions.* Chicago: University of Chicago Press.

Laitin, David D., James A. Caporaso, David Collier, Ronald Rogowski, and Sidney Tarrow. 1995. "Review Symposium: The Qualitative-Quantitative Distinction: Gary King, Robert O. Keohane and Sidney Verba's *Designing Social Inquiry: Scientific Inference in Qualitative Research.*" *American Political Science Review* 89, no. 2 (June): 454–74.

Lane, Ruth. 1990. "Concrete Theory: An Emerging Political Method." *American Political Science Review* 84, no. 3 (September): 927–40.

Lasswell, Harold D. 1945. *Power and Personality.* New York: Viking.

Lave, Charles A., and James G. March. 1975. *An Introduction to Models in the Social Sciences.* New York: Harper and Row.

Lindblom, Charles E. 1990. *Inquiry and Change: The Troubled Attempt to Understand and Shape Society.* New Haven, CT: Yale University Press.

Long, Norton E. [1958] 1962. "The Local Community as an Ecology of Games." In *The Polity,* 139–55. Chicago: Rand McNally. Originally published *American Journal of Sociology* 44 (November 1958): 251–61.

Lowi, Theodore J. 1992. "The State in Political Science: How We Became What We Study." *American Political Science Review* 86, no. 1 (March): 1–7.

March, James G., and Johan P. Olsen. 1984. "The New Institutionalism: Organizational Factors in Political Life." *American Political Science Review* 78, no. 3 (September): 734–49.

Migdal, Joel S. 1988. *Strong Societies and Weak States: State-Society Relations and State Capabilities in the Third World*. Princeton, NJ: Princeton University Press.

Miller, Warren E., and M. Kent Jennings. 1986. *Parties in Transition: A Longitudinal Study of Party Elites and Party Supporters*. New York: Russell Sage Foundation.

Moe, Terry M. 1980. *The Organization of Interests: Incentives and the Internal Dynamics of Political Interest Groups*. Chicago: University of Chicago Press.

Moore, Barrington, Jr. 1966. *The Social Origins of Dictatorship and Democracy*. Boston: Beacon Press.

North, Douglass C., and Robert P. Thomas. 1973. *The Rise of the Western World: A New Economic History*. Cambridge: Cambridge University Press.

Parsons, Talcott. 1951. *The Social System*. New York: The Free Press of Glencoe.

Pitt, Joseph C., ed. 1988. *Theories of Explanation*. New York: Oxford University Press.

Polsby, Nelson W. 1983. *Consequences of Party Reform*. New York: Oxford University Press.

Pressman, Jeffrey L., and Aaron Wildavsky. 1979. *Implementation*. 2d ed. Berkeley: University of California Press.

Przeworski, Adam, and John Sprague. 1986. *Paper Stones: A History of Electoral Socialism*. Chicago: University of Chicago Press.

Ricci, David M. 1984. *The Tragedy of Political Science: Scholarship and Democracy*. New Haven, CT: Yale University Press.

Roelofs, H. Mark. 1994. "Two Ways to Political Science: Critical and Descriptive." *PS: Political Science and Politics* 27, no. 2 (June): 264–68.

Rosecrance, Richard N. 1963. *Action and Reaction in World Politics: International Systems in Perspective*. Westport, CT: Greenwood.

Schelling, Thomas. 1963. *Strategy of Conflict*. New York: Oxford Galaxy.

Seidelman, Raymond, with Edward J. Harpham. 1985. *Disenchanted Realists: Political Science and the American Crisis 1884–1984*. Albany, NY: SUNY Press.

Skowronek, Stephen. 1982. *Building a New American State: The Expansion of National Administrative Capacities 1877–1920*. Cambridge: Cambridge University Press.

———. 1984. "Presidential Leadership in Political Time." In *The Presidency and the Political System,* ed. Michael Nelson, pp. 87–132. Washington, DC: CQ Press.

Smith, Adam. [1776] 1937. *An Inquiry into the Nature and Causes of the Wealth of Nations*. New York: Modern Library.

Suppe, Frederick. 1989. *The Semantic Conception of Theories and Scientific Realism*. Urbana and Chicago: University of Illinois Press.

Waldrop, M. Mitchell. 1992. *Complexity: The Emerging Science at the Edge of Order and Chaos*. New York. Simon and Schuster.

2 CONCRETE THEORY IN POLITICAL SCIENCE

> The task of science . . . is to demystify experience and simplify it,
> not to extol its complexities.
>
> —Kramer 1986, 16

Recognizing Innovation

Every time the president of the United States of America appears in his ceremonial capacity, a band plays "Ruffles and Flourishes" and finally "Hail to the Chief," so that casual visitors, who might inadvertently ignore the great event they are about to witness, may be suitably warned and their attention attracted. It would be a great convenience if something of this sort could be arranged in political science, so that when a new method occurs, a brass band would waken the unwary to the event. At present no such arrangements exist, so that the political audience remains free to ignore or bypass or disdain the appearance of new kinds of theory. This does not at all imply that specific research projects (those interpreted here as examples of concrete theory) have been ignored—quite the opposite, in fact, because the excellence of the works usually attracts a wide and appreciative audience. What is ignored, however, is the theoretic quality of the research.[1]

Innovation is often easiest to recognize in stages, and this principle makes it appropriate to begin discussion of the politics model with a series of studies first identified (Lane 1990) simply as examples of 'concrete theory.' Although it may seem surprising to describe theory as concrete, when it is usually considered inherently abstract, the designation is an apt one. It denotes a kind of theory that, rather than rising above the political process to form conceptual *frameworks* by means of which events can be categorized (Easton 1965; Parsons 1951; Boynton 1980; Coleman 1964; Kemeny and Snell 1978), instead cuts to fundamental behavioral *processes* that underlie political outcomes (Lave and

March 1975; Stinchcombe 1968; Hempel 1965a, 447–53; Harre 1970, 26–28; Harre 1986).

Both types of theory—the 'abstract' and the 'concrete'—may be equally scientific, but they develop their concepts in two quite different ways. The abstract approach mounts from reality to ever higher (and emptier) concepts; the concrete approach equally achieves universality, but it does so not by rising but by burrowing: It strips away all inessential attributes and lays bare a central process that underlies, and serves to explain, observed political events.[2]

Defining Concrete Theory

The concrete approach is no stranger to political science. Early examples of its spirit can be recognized in such well-known works in political science as Barnard's (1938, 46–61) organizational model, Bentley's (1908) political 'process' models, Neustadt's (1980, 131) presidential model, Key's (1964, 200–201) theory of party genesis, Fenno's (1966, 681–88) study of congressional committee dynamics, and Apter's (1972, 415–24) theory of modernization. What these works share is a vigorous grasp of the living political process, unhampered by analytical preconceptions.

A causal next step in the formation of concrete theory, giving a new strength to the direction initiated by these early works, was taken by the classical generation of rational choice theorists (Simon 1945; Downs 1957; Schelling 1963; Buchanan and Tullock 1962; Riker 1962; and Olson 1965). But it is important to understand that rational choice theory and concrete theory are not the same. Concrete theory borrows the logical rigor introduced by the rational choice theorists, but concrete theory's methods and assumptions are both more flexible and more deeply empirical.

Concrete theory is defined by several characteristics that its exemplars share, and that distinguish it from other scientific approaches to the study of politics. While one or two of the elements may be found individually in other works, it is the presence of the *complete cluster* that distinguishes, and serves to define, concrete theory.

The major defining marks of concrete theory include:

1. A focus on actual decision makers, usually political elites, as the object of study; this is in direct contrast both to the survey re-

search emphasis on mass behavior (Campbell, Converse, Miller, and Stokes 1964, 1966) and the institutional approach (Evans, Rueschemeyer, and Skocpol 1985; Tilly 1975).

2. An expanded self-interest axiom that deepens the level of explanation by providing for a variety of political, as distinct from purely economic, goals; the decision makers are neither unreasonably rational nor are they cognitively out of their depth (e.g., Simon 1982; Kahneman, Slovic, and Tversky 1982; Wason and Johnson-Laird 1972).

3. Close attention to the environment, especially the political institutions and the political environment within which decision occurs (Popper 1972, 178–80; Farr 1987).

4. A strong logical quality that vigorously shapes its materials into dynamic models that capture the 'action' of politics; it is this characteristic that gives concrete theory its radically explanatory quality (Merton 1957; Lave and March 1975).

5. An overriding concern with specificity infusing these several features of concrete theory: The cases discussed below, for instance, deal not with institutions in general, but with specific institutions; not behavior in general, but specific types of behavior.

Exemplars of the new brand of concrete theorists may be found in all the subdisciplines within political science: for example, Tullock (1965) on organizational behavior; Sylvan and Chan (1984) on foreign policy decision making; Stewart, Hermann, and Hermann (1989) on Soviet behavior; Dogan and Pelassy (1984, Chapter 10) on clientalism; Liebenow (1986) on civilian–military relations; Jacobs (1970) on the dynamics of city growth.

The present chapter focuses on eight examples of concrete theorizing, taken from all political research subfields, that illustrate the way the approach can be applied successfully to a broad range of political phenomena. The works include Bates (1981) on African economic leadership; Jacobson and Kernell (1983) on congressional voting; Miller and Jennings (1986) on presidential party conventions; North and Thomas (1973) on political-economic development; Przeworski and Sprague (1986) on electoral socialism; Skowronek (1984) on presidential decision making; Pressman and Wildavsky (1979) on public program failure; and George and Smoke (1974) on international deterrence theory.[3]

It might be said that it is premature to discuss a methodology that has not been explicitly defined by its practitioners, but the alternative argument is stronger: The problem with concrete theory is that it is easily lost. Several of the concrete theorists included here have written works that do not display the attributes of concrete theory (e.g., Bates 1983; Jennings 1981; Kernell 1986; contrast, however, Jacobson 1980 and perhaps Przeworski 1985). This situation emphasizes the need to make an explicit definition at this time.

Because introduction of a new idea proceeds best through actual examples, readers may prefer to skip at this point directly to the discussion of the specific works. For those who choose to have a proper introduction, the next section briefly frames concrete theory within the philosophy of science, social science theory, and the practice of political research. The criteria for concrete theory are reevaluated in the closing sections, and a well-known survey of the discipline (March and Olsen 1984) is used to suggest that concrete theory contains elements of behavioralism and institutionalism in what may be a happy blend.

Science and Theory

The appropriate canvas against which to evaluate new developments in empirical theory is not, at the start, the philosophy of science but the methodology of the social sciences.[4] Among the most important issues here has been the attention given by positivist philosophers of science to theory *testing* as the criterion by which science is separated from nonscience (Popper 1959; Lakatos 1970; Kuhn 1962). Though this course was justified historically by the changed direction taken in political science (Easton 1953; Eulau 1963; Macridis 1955; Dahl 1963), and retains its importance (Almond 1988, 872), the singleminded focus on theory testing alone is no longer a complete solution to the development of political science. As Ball argues, the attention to theory rejection can become obsessive. Political scientists, rather than giving research programs a fighting chance, "have made them into sitting ducks; and, in a discipline which includes many accomplished duck hunters, this has often proved fatal" (Ball 1987, 34).

In trying actually to build empirical theories, political scientists have had little practical assistance; what literature exists is found largely in the neighboring social sciences rather than in political science itself. I review briefly here some ideas germane to the problem, from a very short list of books about the practice of empirical theorizing (Merton 1957; Glaser and Strauss 1967; Stinchcombe 1968; Lave and March 1975) in order to provide a methodological framework within which concrete theory can be viewed.

The most familiar point at which to start is Robert Merton's often cited, yet rarely studied, "theories of the middle range" (Merton 1957, 5–10). Merton was a strong supporter of the idea of theory-guided research, yet 'grand theory' was anathema to him—the epithet he uses is "grandiose." This appears to be a position with which many political scientists, chastened by events of the past decades, might concur. Is there an alternative to grand theory?

Merton defined his alternative choice, middle-range theory, as "intermediate to the minor working hypotheses evolved in abundance during day-to-day routines of research, and the all-inclusive speculations comprising a master conceptual scheme" (Merton 1957, 5–6). Middle-range theories develop stepwise, as "special theories adequate to limited ranges of social data" are consolidated into "groups of special theories" in which individual theories' inconsistencies have been ironed out, the premises clarified, and the logical connections made explicit (Merton 1957, 10, 14–15).

While no parallel can be wholly exact, Merton's description of middle-range theory is wholly compatible with concrete theory.[5] The subjects over which the explanation ranges are many, and the theory therefore has a wide scope. But it is not universal in the sense we have come to associate with 'grand' theory, of attempting to build frameworks within which every possible event can be contained (compare Verba 1985, 34, on "islands of theory" as preferable to "too general" theory).

While avoiding grand theory, however, it is important not to lose the theoretical quality itself. The attempt to avoid all abstract concepts, as found in Glaser and Strauss's "grounded theory" (1967, 259–62), may throw the baby out with the bath. But the idea of grounded theory is useful here, in demarcating the field in which concrete theory exists. Concrete theory as it is delineated here would not be better theory if it were more concrete; rather, it would degenerate into isolated concepts lacking the logical interconnectedness characteristic of Merton's brand of theory.

Levels of Theory

The broadest viewpoint on theory is provided by a sociologist amply known to political scientists, Arthur Stinchcombe (1968). His particular contribution to our search for an understanding of empirical theory is found in his schematization of the field in terms of the various levels of abstraction, or generality, involved. This is useful because, as Stinchcombe notes, many quarrels over theory are actually debates over "the level of generality it is fruitful to work at" rather than over the theories themselves (Stinchcombe 1968, 47).

Stinchcombe's description of the various levels of generality at which theories can be built (1968, 48–50) can be abbreviated; but giving all seven points is necessary because only by seeing the full range of possible levels can one clearly see where a specific type of theory might fit. Stinchcombe's classification is summarized below: The terminology has been modified to simplify the condensed presentation, but the examples are his own. The order is from most general to most specific.

1. Metaphysical assumptions about materialism–idealism, valid forms of logical inference, and causal premises.
2. Broad "schools" (e.g., functionalism, Freudian theory, Marxism).
3. Important concepts within each school (e.g., unconscious behavior, property relations).
4. For each conceptualization structure, the logical linkages between concepts (e.g., control of behavior by unconscious drives, or by relations of production).
5. Explanations of specific subareas within the general theory (e.g., hysterical paresis, Bonapartism).
6. Derivation of the specific empirical results expected if a theory (point 5) is correct.
7. Evaluation of empirical results. Whether observations support predictions.

The shift from positivism to scientific realism (introduced in Chapter 1 and discussed more thoroughly in Chapter 6) can be understood in its full implications with the help of Stinchcombe's hierarchy, which shows that such a change is properly sited not at subordinate levels but at the very uppermost level, level 1, and thus serves to redefine every level of theory beneath it, from 'schools' to 'empirical evaluation.' In Stinchcombe's terms, the politics model would be at the second-highest level, defining (as outlined in Chapter 3) a model of general political behavior based on a unique pattern of explanatory principles. This politics model is then worked out in detail at levels 4 and 5 by specific concrete theories about specific aspects of political behavior.

One final point may be touched before proceeding to the examples of concrete theory. This is the evolving idea of 'situational analysis' (Nelson 1975; Donagan 1964). Derived from Popper (1972, 179–82), the situational model has been most recently defined within a political context by Farr as a

> detailed description of (1) the natural environment; (2) the social environment (that is, other strategic actors and the social relations between actors), and (3) the problem-situation in which an actor finds himself or herself, defines his or her problems, and tries out tentative solutions. (Farr 1987, 50)

That such a description is congruent with concrete theory will become clear from the examples included in the following section. The parallel adds fuel to my argument that the concrete theories identified here are not merely eccentric appearances within political science, but in fact represent an important new methodological direction (see Watkins 1970; Wisdom 1970).[6]

I turn now to the concrete theorists themselves. Most will be familiar to readers; the only novelty is in the seeing them as a group, unified by a methodological perspective.

Examples of Concrete Theories

Concrete theories are not difficult to summarize. Indeed, one of their most engaging qualities is their simplicity. Though some forms of theory require a considerable commitment of time and memory before one can appreciate their often subtle meaning, concrete theory is short and neat. Therein it fulfills a common methodological requirement for theory, one rarely met by other political theories, that they shall by their simplicity enable researchers better to order and explain their data (Dogan and Pelassy 1984; Kramer 1986).

Jacobson and Kernell

In *Strategy and Choice in Congressional Elections* (1983), Jacobson and Kernell address one of political science's central concerns, the question of why voters vote as they do. The larger issue in this field has been the rationality, or at least the common sense, of the American voter (initially Campbell et al. 1964; Key 1966). The immediate question posed by Jacobson and Kernell is narrowly defined, involving a paradox in empirical studies of voting behavior between aggregate-level data which indicate that voters vote according to economic (and/or political) conditions, and individual-level survey data which show voters making decisions on a variety of personalistic and local grounds.[7]

It is to politically active elites, their strategic behavior, and their roles as connecting links between national conditions and individual voter choice, that Jacobson and Kernell turn to resolve the questions raised by the apparent conflicts in the data. Their 'strategic politicians' theory argues that officeholders, challengers, party leaders, and financial backers all make personal utility calculations about upcoming elections based on national economic and political conditions early in the election year. Good times draw out highly qualified candidates, as well as large financial contributions and strong organizational efforts; in bad times, everyone keeps a low profile and makes only token campaign gestures (Jacobson and Kernell 1983, 20–23).

> National events and conditions shape the expectations of potential candidates and their supporters about their party's electoral prospects. Their expectations affect their strategies and thus their behavior. And this, in turn, structures the choices voters are offered. . . . (Jacobson and Kernell 1983, 24)

> The net result is to so structure choices between candidates across the districts that voters observing campaigns and evaluating candidates will, ceteris paribus, come to prefer the candidates whose party enjoys the structural advantages derived from the various elite strategies. (Jacobson and Kernell 1983, 87)

> . . . [E]ven voters untouched by national events and conditions can thus contribute to national tides by responding to strictly local, seemingly idiosyncratic cues. . . . (Jacobson and Kernell 1983, 71)

In sum, the voters believe (indeed correctly) that they are merely 'voting for the best person,' while in fact national economic and political conditions have determined the outcome.[8]

On the question of parties and their role in the American political system, Jacobson and Kernell draw from their analysis a conclusion that is nonorthodox. They do not join those who complain of the loose American party system, or those who regret its recent 'decline.' Jacobson and Kernell suggest that the failure to meet the strong two-party parliamentary ideal is not necessarily a weakness.

> Offices and elections in America constitute a stable political marketplace within which entrepreneurial politicians can pursue long-term investment strategies. . . . [T]he national vote is a function of many private exchange calculations, including those made by candidates and their supporters; the pyramidal stratification of offices emphasizes that scarcity increases value; political resources are distributed unevenly; and a demand-price mechanism operates. (Jacobson and Kernell 1983, 86)

The degree to which the market mechanism actually prevails is of course an open question. But strategic politicians theory opens a new perspective by utilizing a dynamic approach to the processes underlying party behavior.

African Agricultural Problems

Economists steadfastly retain the faith, as Bates points out in his introduction to *Markets and States in Tropical Africa* (1981), that given the appropriate incentives, peasants in underdeveloped countries will "turn sand into gold." This faith has been severely strained by the results of postcolonial developments. Where development theorists (Almond and Coleman 1960; Apter 1965; Chilcote 1981, 272–87; Janos 1986) believed modernization was a process characterized by a certain inevitability, given the knowledge available to guide the new nations, the actual outcome has been political disarray and economic regression (see the reflections by World Bank advisers in Meier and Seers 1984 and Meier 1987).

Bates's solution to the question of how this result has so universally occurred is sufficiently compact that it deserves to be quoted in his own words.

Fledgling industries locate in the urban areas. Workers and owners, while struggling with each other for their share of industrial profits, possess a common interest in perpetuating policies that increase these profits. They therefore demand policies that shelter and protect these industries. They also demand policies that promise low-cost food.

Because of the public purposes they espouse, African states seek to advance the interests of industry. To secure revenues to promote industry, they therefore seek taxes from agriculture. By maintaining a sheltered industrial order, they generate economic benefits for elites, as well as resources for winning the political backing of influential groups in the urban centers. (Bates 1981, 120)

For the benefit of others, [the farmers] are subjected to policies that violate their interests. But the effects of these policies are increasingly harmful to everyone. Reducing the incentives to grow food leads to reduced food production; the result is higher food prices and waves of discontent in the urban centers. . . . (Bates 1981, 129)

As Bates notes, the logic is "simple but powerful": Urban elements (business and labor) demand protection of their enterprises, and low-cost food to decrease the strain on wages. Governments respond to these interests because they must do so to stay in office, but in keeping agricultural prices low, and agricultural taxes high, they destroy the farmers' incentives to produce. Thus the short-term needs of political elites cause them to adopt practices that in the long run destroy them. Bates uses standard economic analysis to support this theory, but validation in fact requires little more than opening a newspaper.

What is diagnostically concrete about Bates's strategy here is that he does not, as do most researchers, isolate specific sectors of the political situation, such as economics or leadership problems, and treat only one at a time, independently (on African leadership compare recently the approach of Bienen and Van de Walle 1989). Instead, Bates combines all the factors at once, the economic, political, institutional, personal, and so on, linking them by a tight sinuous logic that arranges each factor in a dialectic relation to each of the other factors. This strategy succeeds because it resists the push toward universality, the temptation to dilute the message by including *all* values of every variable. A sharp choice is made, in line with Occam's Razor, eliminating secondary factors toward the goal of creating a vivid model of the central process.

Przeworski and Sprague

Students of socialism have sometimes despaired of finding any scientific hard ground in a subject area covered by the marshes of ideology. The third example of concrete theory, *Paper Stones* (Przeworski and Sprague 1986), stands as an exception. The book (the title of which reflects the early socialist belief that ballots would supersede violence as a path to socialism) centers on one of the most vehemently debated questions in the socialist literature—the possibility of a "parliamentary road to socialism," that is, a peaceful revolution.

The topic has been approached two ways: through the Marxist polemical literature, which is both deductive and normative (Gramsci 1971; Lukacs 1971), and through the field of comparative voting studies (Lipset 1960; Rose 1980). Przeworski and Sprague take neither of these routes. Their strategy is one which will by now be recognized as typical of concrete theory, the development of middle-range theory focused on elites and their independent, dynamic role in the political process.[9]

The theoretic aspect of their voting analysis results from a perspective that defines the voting decision as a result of elite behavior rather than of simple demographic factors. The formative element that shapes objective conditions into politically relevant conditions is the political parties. The party elites shape the nature of the political argument: The salience of any socioeconomic factor, such as class, is a "cumulative consequence of the strategies pursued by political parties" (Przeworski and Sprague 1986, 9).

Despite the political generality of this theory as an explanation of total political systems, *Paper Stones* employs it only as it relates to the central topic, electoral socialism. For parties of the left, the attempt to shape the objective factors into workable political form is irresolvable because the existence of socialist parties ameliorates the condition of the workers, and the better conditions become, the less urgent is the need for socialism (Przeworski and Sprague 1986, 1–11). The centerpiece of the book is a formal model incorporating the dynamics of this dilemma; the empirical data, while difficult, tend to confirm the model (Przeworski and Sprague 1986, 174).

The broader implications of the Przeworski–Sprague model are brought out in the epilogue, which challenges both those who seek to reduce politics to economics, and those who seek to reduce it to society or culture (1986, 182). Voters cannot be explained by simple demographic factors, but are influenced by "the totality of social relations." These social relations, in turn, are shaped by elite strategies: "The causes of individual voting behavior are produced in the course of history by conflicting political forces," not only by parties, but by unions, schools, religions, and other institutions (Przeworski and Sprague 1986, 7, 143).

North and Thomas

The Rise of the Western World, by North and Thomas (1973), is an oddly thin book; the topic would seem to call for greater tonnage. The book's size results partially from its being, according to the authors, an 'agenda' rather than an exhaustive study; yet the method employed is also a reason. Concrete theorists typically strip subjects to essentials.

The work begins with a question that has often been slighted: Why do some societies 'fail'? By the seventeenth century, Holland and England were flourishing, France was second-rate, Spain and Italy were "losers" (North and Thomas 1973, 103–15). Economics provides a preliminary answer: "Efficient economic organization is the key to growth," and efficiency occurs when property rights are so organized that the opportunity for private (personal) gain leads people to undertake activities that entail social gains as well. The decisive political question is under what circumstances do governments organize property rights efficiently (North and Thomas 1973, 1–3)?

Historically, property rights are inextricably linked to kings and taxes. As Europe emerged from its feudal period, kings needed money to pay armies that no longer could be filled by vassals. Since all government "is primarily an institutional arrangement that sells protection and justice to its constituents" and receives taxes in return, the central problem for monarchs was how best to raise the money necessary to carry out these tasks. Kings were trying to survive, not to plan ahead (North and Thomas 1973, 97, 100).

The political dynamics of the North and Thomas model arise from the specific circumstances and problems faced by the sovereigns in the various European states: (1) the structure of the economy (international trade is easier to tax than domestic trade, for instance); (2) the vigor of the political competition (England did not face challenges such as the Dukes of Burgundy posed to the French throne, for instance); (3) the constituents' gains from central government (greater in centralized France than in decentralized England, where order was maintained at the local level). Within these constraints, kings and parliaments bargained for control. Monarchs who needed too much money too fast (oversized government or personal luxury or war) found it tempting to leave inefficient feudal taxes in place, and modern economic relationships failed to come to the fore. Where government was highly administered and therefore expensive, heavy taxes stifled development.

The North–Thomas model is by no means as amenable to empirical testing as have been the examples of concrete theory discussed previously, and the historical materials the authors provide stimulate the appetite for empirical evidence more than they satisfy it. Nevertheless, North and Thomas extend the reach of the methodology by employing it on historical questions crucial to the understanding of present-day problems of economic and political development.

Presidential Decision Making

Stephen Skowronek's "Presidential Leadership in Political Time" (1984) is somewhat different from other examples of concrete theory presented here, in that it does not illuminate an interaction among several elite decision makers but rather deals with single actors—that is, U.S. presidents.[10] However, the interactive focus is implicit: For Skowronek, the president plays a kind of 'game against nature' where the era's whole political-institutional structure serves to define 'nature.'

The starting point of Skowronek's study is the natural but often overlooked question of why specific presidents behave as they do in office.

> Presidential leadership often is pictured as a contest between the man and the system. Timeless forces of political fragmentation and institutional intransigence threaten to frustrate the would-be leader at every turn. Success is reserved for the exceptional individual. . . .
>
> Although the significance of the particular person in office cannot be doubted, this perspective . . . tends to obscure differences in the political situations in which [individual incumbents] act. If presidential leadership is indeed something of a struggle between the individual and the system, it must be recognized that the system changes as well as the incumbent. The changing universe of political action is an oft-noted but seldom explored dimension of the leadership problem. (Skowronek 1984, 127)

To appreciate the unusual nature of such an approach requires only a nodding acquaintance with the mainstream presidential literature, which with some exceptions is characterized by the timeless, idealized 'textbook president' (outlined in Cronin 1980), or by the modern equivalent of the 'advice to princes' tradition. Skowronek's nonjudgmental approach is in sharp contrast to these normative perspectives, although it is not without forebears (Neustadt 1980; Barber 1977).

The Skowronek thesis is that a political system is characterized by institutional cycles, made up of stages of construction, maintenance, and decline; and that individual presidents can only be understood in the light of the strategies they espouse in response to the specific situation they face. Though there are other cyclical or time-anchored theories (Barber 1980; Hargrove and Nelson 1984), Skowronek differs in the focus on elites, rather than on, say, psychological cycles of innovation and fatigue in the electorate.

Political periods "are marked by the rise to power of new political coalitions, with one, in particular, exerting a dominant influence over the federal government." But in the course of history, each coalition decays internally because of "conflicts among interests within the dominant coalition"; national problems and needs change as well. Increasingly the regime depends for support upon "sectarian interests with myopic demands." The longer it survives, the more it is enervated and unable to cope with current problems (Skowronek 1984, 87–88).

Presidents (or regime leaders) therefore face three typical situations, which recur cyclically over time: (1) the challenge of regime construction (Jackson and FDR); (2) the problem of regime maintenance and control of conflict (Polk and Kennedy); and (3) the necessity for establishing leadership in an enervated regime (Pierce and Carter) (Skowronek 1984, 89). Skowronek evaluates each of the three pairs of presidents according to this theory, and is able to show how the outcome of each administration was structured by its institutional circumstances.

Miller and Jennings

Parties in Transition (1986), by Miller and Jennings, is rich in empirical results. Indeed, the very scope of the empirical analysis is apt to obscure the important way in which the authors take a fundamentally different approach from earlier studies of national party elites: Their interest is less the actors in isolation, and more the institutions within which the actors are enmeshed.

Parties in Transition begins as a replication of earlier studies of national party presidential convention delegates (Kirkpatrick 1976). This level of analysis is itself innovative, in moving away from the party-in-the-electorate approach and the pervasive influence of theories of party realignment (see the excellent survey in Petrocik 1981).

Though the importance of the candidate is a truism with which few would quarrel (Asher 1984; Kessel 1980), it has rarely been connected dynamically to elite behavior, or the elite's impact on campaign and therefore electoral behavior.[11] The Miller–Jennings study showed that individual presidential candidates made a "decisive contribution" to the behavior of party activists, who tended to be brought into the political process, and to define themselves, in terms of specific candidates (Miller and Jennings 1986, 19–20). The parties are seen not as unified but as deeply fissured.

The innovation of Miller and Jennings is to define the internal processes of political parties as based on the highly personal interaction of specific political people. Rather than presenting national conventions as part of a grand, orderly process, or as a more or less abstract scramble for political profit, many of Miller and Jennings's findings related more "to the somewhat idiosyncratic fates of particular candidacies" than to the structural aspects of the two-party system (1986, 19–20). Asked their motivations for entering the political process, by all odds the outstanding answer (at 94–97 percent, well ahead of policies, partisanship, or careerism) was "to elect particular candidates" (1986, 93–94). "From our survey of possible causes for circulation of people into and out of the ranks of campaign activists, it is clear that candidates play a central role . . ." (Miller and Jennings 1986, 19).

It is especially interesting that the authors document persuasively the existence of strong ideological differences *within* the parties.

> The coalitions we observed [within each party] were not simply the result of certain candidates exuding great personal charm, or of party or interest group leaders playing the role of power brokers. Rather the groupings stand for *basic divisions of thought* about matters of public policy and the political process. Like-minded campaign activists, mainly through a process of self-selection, gather around attractive candidates who ostensibly share their ideological views. (Miller and Jennings 1986, 247; emphasis added)

The exact shape of these ideologies, and the way they define intraparty struggles, is not further probed in the Miller and Jennings study. But their work strongly hints that a full understanding of political parties will not be possible until more is known about the attitudes and values that characterize the 'subparties.'

Policy Implementation

Pressman and Wildavsky (1979) were not the first to notice that public programs fail, but their study is unusual because it takes failure at its full seriousness. The Oakland Project, initiated in 1965 by the Economic Development Administration to improve economic opportunities in the city of Oakland, began, as the authors describe in detail, with widespread national and community support. It ended in collapse; one sector of the program elicited the unhappy headline, "US Invests $1,085,000 To Create 43 Oakland Jobs" (Pressman and Wildavsky 1979, 82). While this was not the whole picture, neither was it altogether misleading.

The model developed by the authors in the course of the Oakland analysis centers on (1) the elite groups involved in the Oakland program, (2) their widely diverse goals, (3) the unexpected obstacles caused by the interactive process between actors and their goals, and (4) the logic of program breakdown. The authors are at pains to emphasize that the Oakland Project was not controversial; no local opposition existed to EDA's plans, and the program was "everyday" and "prosaic" in character (1979, 93). This serves to highlight the eventual failure.

Though there was no overt controversy, the participants, including several federal agencies, local politicians, and local businesspeople, were subtly different: Some desired a showcase success in reducing unemployment, others sought business opportunities, others were concerned with fiscal regularity and efficiency, and so on (1979, 95–97). Ends and means became entangled:

> As the managers of each program try to impose their preferred sequence of events on the others, their priorities for the next step, which differs for each one and cannot be equally important to all, may conflict. The means loom larger all the time because they are what the action is about. Actually, it is easier to disagree about means because they are there to provoke quarrels, while ends are always around the corner. (Pressman and Wildavsky 1979, 98–99)

Pressman and Wildavsky consider this not pernicious but natural. "Allow enough time to elapse in a rapidly changing external world and it is hard to imagine any set of agreements remaining firm" (1979, 92). And this occurred despite EDA's vigorous efforts to achieve unity and coordination on the noncontroversial project. Programs fail for no apparent reason,

> . . . because we do not begin to appreciate the number of steps involved, the number of participants whose preferences have to be taken into account, the number of separate decisions that are part of what we think of as a single one. Least of all do we appreciate the geometric growth of interdependencies over time where each negotiation involves a number of participants with decisions to make, whose implications ramify over time. (Pressman and Wildavsky 1979, 93)

In their interpretation of program administration as inescapably political, Pressman and Wildavsky include, somewhat as a by-product, a devastating criticism of functional theory. We are deceived in reasoning backward from what exists, they argue.

> Looking back at the very array of governmental programs that are in operation, we conclude that they must have been implemented. Why, then, should our new program fail in implementation when so many others that fill the landscape have evidently succeeded? It is easy to forget (perhaps because we never knew) about their initial difficulties. The years of trial and error that led to the present state of operation are lost from view. . . . Programs that started out to accomplish one set of objectives end up accomplishing another for which, long after the fact, we give undue credit for implementation. (Pressman and Wildavsky 1979, 113, 116)

Deterrence Theory

The concluding example of concrete theory comes from the field of international politics and is distinctive in its explicit recognition that its methodology fits none of the usual categories. George and Smoke (1974) describe their work in deterrence theory as both historical and inductive, and contrast it with two familiar alternative methodologies: "abstract deductivist" theory, which they find misleading, and "statistical-correlational" analysis, which they find disappointing (1974, 503, 513,

88). They also distinguish their approach from case studies (92–94). In the course of analyzing a wide array of foreign policy cases, including the 1948 Berlin blockade, the outbreak of the Korean War and Chinese intervention, the Hungarian revolution, the Eisenhower Doctrine in the Middle East, and the 1962 Cuban Missile Crisis, the authors criticize Cold War deterrence theory not only for its excessive simplification but for its excessive emphasis on threat and punishment.

In the stead of such narrower approaches they propose to revise deterrence theory into a more widely applicable 'influence theory,' covering multilateral strategic interactions of both a positive and negative nature.

> . . . [W]hat is needed is not merely a better deterrence theory per se but rather a broader theory which encompasses deterrence as one of a number of means that can be employed, separately or in some combination, to influence conflict processes and to control the conflict potential in inter-state relations. (George and Smoke 1974, 591)

Their new deterrence model involves two conceptual actors, the 'defender,' who is trying to maintain the status quo, and the 'initiator' of the crisis, who is trying to change that status. The interaction of these two actors within the crisis situation is defined by three conceptual stages—commitment, initiation, and response—each of which is linked to the others in a dynamic algorithmic, or 'iterative,' flow (George and Smoke 1974, 550, 98–102). Traditional deterrence theory, as the authors note, works primarily with only the first of these stages (1974, 551).

The dynamics of the model are shown most clearly in the final or 'response' stage. The defending actor, once some challenge has been made, must tailor its response carefully to take into account not only strategic factors but cognitive and domestic political factors as well (George and Smoke 1974, 581). If this is not done, and the action taken by the initiator is misperceived, the defender runs the risk that its response may exacerbate rather than reduce tensions: A strong response, which might stop one initiator, may cause another initiator to escalate the conflict (1974, 577). This need for mutual assessment by the two players, requiring that each have an accurate 'image' of the other, evokes George's earlier work on operational codes (George and Smoke 1974, 582–83).

When the three phases are seen altogether, the process of deterrence can be described in a flow chart (George and Smoke 1974, 98–102) in which the two actors cyclically estimate each other's intentions and actions, engage in interaction, and revise their estimates and possibly their goals and commitments as the action develops (1974, 579). This of course brings the deterrence model near to the boundary of a general political interaction model.

Classifying Concrete Theory

What can be said about concrete theory that will 'situate' it, that will throw light on its nature and functions? We have seen earlier that concrete theories, while obviously directed to empirical phenomena of the most 'concrete' sort, do not fit the usual varieties of empiricism, are neither statistical-correlational nor abstract deductivist. It is also superficially obvious that concrete theories, coming from the very heart of mainstream political science, are not critical in the sense of, say, the Frankfurt School. Concrete theories, finally, seem not opposed to the norms of natural science, and take no account of the hermeneutic argument against objectivism in social science. These difficulties of classification suggest the usefulness of a second look at the defining characteristics of concrete theory.

In considering, in retrospect, the cluster of attributes by which concrete theory could be recognized, deeper familiarity with actual concrete theories makes plain that the most obvious of the attributes is not the most important. The attention to elites will remain a convenient diagnostic tool and perhaps even serve as a guide to research, yet it is a kind of historical artifact. Elites take on importance in concrete models only because true political interaction can occur only within relatively compact groups. The real subject of concrete theory is any group of persons who are engaged in the making of important governmental decisions. If direct democracy were feasible, the approach would study masses rather than elites.

In terms of the core of concrete methodology, the attribute that is of fundamental importance is 'process,' the direct interaction of two or more political individuals. Process summarizes the other characteristics because it entails the political interaction of persons with (1) a broad array of social, economic, and political motives, and (2) highly varied resources to bring to bear on the attainment of their goals. The concrete models presented here have described varieties of motivation far beyond the simple political economy models. The motivations ranged from the problems of achieving and retaining public office in several types of political systems (North and Thomas, Bates, Jacobson and Kernell), to overthrowing officeholders (Przeworski and Sprague), to problems of governing (Skowronek), policy formulation (Miller and Jennings, George and Smoke), and policy implementation (Pressman and Wildavsky). It is the intersection of these variegated motives that provides dynamism to the models discussed here.

Politics and Process

The integration of the environment in concrete models may appear somewhat indefinite. Three types of environment appeared in the models described here: economic conditions, social structure, and political institutions. The socioeconomic factors were interrelated: interest groups defined according to economic location (Bates), economic stratifications determining attitudes to reform or revolution (Przeworski and Sprague), and taxation as a function of who is economically available for taxation, and who is socially vulnerable to it (North and Thomas). The political environment included the coalition structure within which policy is made (Skowronek), the nature and range of the political preferences in the electorate that constrain the nominating process (Miller and Jennings), the impact of 'interests' on broad policy agreements (Pressman and Wildavsky), the evaluation of what makes 'good' candidates (Jacobson and Kernell), and geopolitical questions of position and status (George and Smoke).

This rather complex set of environmental factors can be summarized conveniently under the rubric of actor 'resources.' The resources may be economic (wealth or natural resources), social (the number and type of allies), political (the holding of particular offices with associated rights and duties), or strategic (simple 'location' in the field). The nature of the resource distribution is directly tied to the motivations, of course. Those actors who have resources wish to keep them; those actors who lack resources wish to acquire them; and those that have some, but not enough, resources, enter the political process with other actors of similarly mixed motives in order to negotiate those political outcomes that constitute the "authoritative allocation of values."

The dynamic concept of process knits all these elements together in an orderly way. The core of the concrete method, from an analytic rather than a descriptive viewpoint, is composed of a series of 'n' actors, each of which acts on the basis of its aims (desire for office, for power, for peace, for wealth) and is helped or hindered by having, or not having, resources (money, or office, or eloquence). Both aims and resources are defined by the environment because the environment decides the range of the options (e.g., 'This is not a good year for Democrats') and the resources (e.g., 'Your oil pipelines run through our territory, and your vulnerability is our resource'). This is a familiar enough paradigm; what is unusual about the concrete theorists is the verve with which they employ it to unlock everyday political problems. While historians may provide similar factual material, the clearly defined logic of the concrete models enables the observer to see not only 'how it hangs together,' but how facts, properly arranged, become theory.[12]

This pattern recalls an earlier work, the volume edited by Parsons and Shils (1951), *Toward a General Theory of Action,* so influential in the early phases of behavioralism, and so little studied today. Its approach is much more 'theoretical' than the concrete theories presented here, but is also very similar to them in its emphasis on individual actors, goals, and interaction in an environment. The goal of the work, which did not share the macrosystems approach of Parsons's other work, was to be objective about subjective factors. As Bauman outlines it, Parsons's problem was

> . . . to construct a model of social action which could be, simultaneously, an object of understanding as a subjective, meaningful phenomenon, and an object of scientific theory, as a model amenable to objective analysis. . . . The obvious way of doing this is to postulate the actor's motives as the decisive causal factor in selecting both ends and means. . . . (Bauman 1978, 133–34)

Concrete theorists' 'solution' to the problem of positivism is intrinsically similar to that of Parsons. We look over the shoulders of the participants, we see the problem as they see it, we comprehend their actions in the light of their own understandings. The concrete theorist transcends the individual perspectives, however, because the model demands that not just one, but all, perspectives be included. It is this that gives concrete methodology its 'objective' aspect.

Evaluation of Concrete Theory

Evaluation of the thesis that concrete theory is both a new and a viable approach to political science's questions demands satisfaction on two points, novelty and viability. I deal with them in turn.

Though as a general rule, defining a scientific 'mainstream' is difficult unless real revolution is in the air (Easton 1965; Macridis 1955), which is not the case here, a recent analysis comes very near to achieving such a description. It will serve as a yardstick in attempting to locate and to evaluate concrete theory.

The masterly summary and critique by March and Olsen (1984) is especially useful because it provides not only an analytic overview of political science since the 1950s, but also its major contemporary challenger, the "new institutionalism." By defining these two frameworks with precision, March and Olsen allow us to compare concrete theory with both of its alternatives, and thereby to answer our first question, the authenticity of the claim that concrete theory is truly original. I briefly outline the differences March and Olsen find between the two schools, then comment in sequence on concrete theory's position in respect to each. The comparison shows that concrete theory is not consistent either with behavioralism or with the "new institutionalism," but has footholds in both camps and links them.

Concrete theory's originality appears to result from two characteristics. First, concrete theory is individualistic, as is behavioralism, but concrete analyses are directed to a different category of politically active individuals—elites rather than citizens. Second, concrete theory is, in every case described above, wholly embedded in an institutional perspective. This is not to say concrete theory straddles the disciplinary fence, borrowing a bit here, an opposite bit there, condemning itself to a verdict of opportunism or eclecticism. Rather, concrete theory tends to show that the polarities are not as distinct as they have seemed. A point-by-point comparison illustrates this conclusion.

Differences Between Schools

March and Olsen contrast behavioralism and institutionalism on five dimensions (1984, 735–40).

1. Contextualism: Behavioralism considers the polity integral to society, with little independence of this environmental context; in-

stitutionalism defines the state as independent, acting upon society as an autonomous force.

2. Reductionism: Behavioralism assumes that collective behavior can be reduced to, and explained by, individual behavior; institutionalism sees institutions acting (through individuals) to ensure satisfaction of institutional needs.

3. Utilitarianism: Behavioralism defines rational actors as persons who calculate their actions to maximize their utility in uncertain but flexible environments; institutionalism emphasizes the importance of constraints imposed on individuals by rules, expectations, traditions.

4. Functionalism: Behavioralism de-emphasizes historical factors and works for "efficient" equilibriums; institutionalism has greater faith in the recalcitrance of historical events and in the constraints imposed by history in reaching solutions.

5. Instrumentalism: Behavioralism sees symbols as irrelevant or exploitative; institutionalism understands symbols as educational and creative of purpose and political identity.

In regard to March and Olsen's first element, "contextualism," concrete theories include both the idea of the autonomy of state officials, who actively structure the political arena, and the idea of the close links between those officials and society at large, which is the source of constraints and opportunities (see especially Jacobson and Kernell; Przeworski and Sprague; Skowronek; Pressman and Wildavsky).

The criterion of 'reductionism' similarly shows that concrete theory partakes of both the behavioralist and the institutionalist perspectives. Concrete theorists, as described above, both reduce and do not reduce: They explain aggregate behavior as the result of individual decisions, but these individuals are not abstractions such as economic man. Rather they are different sorts of persons, each grouping of which is defined by its role in some political or institutional process (see Bates; Miller and Jennings; Przeworski and Sprague; George and Smoke).

'Utilitarianism' again puts concrete theorists on both sides: Concrete theory's decision makers are rational strategic calculators; however, they calculate not in isolation but as the players of roles defined by institutions, norms, expectations, and history (see Skowronek; Miller and Jennings; Przeworski and Sprague; George and Smoke; Pressman and Wildavsky).

The conclusion is the same in reference to 'functionalism': Concrete theory sometimes finds equilibria (of which some are negative equilibria), but in other cases history cannot be escaped, and breakdown occurs before goals are reached. (Contrast Jacobson and Kernell, where the rise and fall of the economy, in conjunction with the goals of party elites, may create stable alternating patterns, with Bates, where the logic of urban-rural dynamics leads steadily downhill.)

Finally, the role of symbols again links concrete theory to both sides of the disciplinary divide: Concrete theorists 'discover' that elites manipulate symbols, but this manipulation is done for a complicated range of purposes, at least some of which entail good public policy. And though they would not seem to deny that symbols are elite-serving, the concrete theorists affirm the importance of such symbols in defining the long-term life of the polity (e.g., Skowronek; Przeworski and Sprague; Miller and Jennings).

Evaluation

In reviewing these comparisons between concrete theory and the behavioral and institutional traditions defined by March and Olsen (1984), we develop a modest confidence in asserting that a type of theory which fits into neither of the major traditions of political science must be accorded a prima facie claim to originality. And a kind of theory that partakes of both traditions cannot be said to be lacking relevance. If concrete theory is indeed new, it is not unfamiliar to political scientists.

The question of viability remains. Perhaps the most severe disability from which concrete theory suffers is that it may not be recognized as theory. Because concrete theory is deeply set in realistic problems and contexts, it may appear too close to 'journalistic' description and for this reason not be treated with sufficient seriousness. Even the authors themselves may seek greater formality and technical sophistication, thereby losing the dynamic, explanatory quality characteristic of middle-range theory.

Data acquisition may also become a problem for concrete theory, since data on the behavior of elites are not readily available. Elites are often difficult to approach, resistant to candid revelation, and very likely innocent about their own political motives (see Fenno 1978, Appendix). The examples of concrete theory show that it is by no means fully developed as a methodology, and, as indicated above, each individual concrete analysis raises as many questions as it answers.[13]

Concrete theory and the politics model combine classical questions of political science with a methodology unique to political science. Together they suggest we can make bolder use of existing materials and enrich our ability to understand both the broader perspectives of politics and the immediate, perplexing practical problems faced by nation and world (Pye 1968). Historically, political scientists have tended to avert their eyes from exactly those 'political' questions that one would have thought would be their highest concern (Ricci 1984). Concrete theorists reverse this direction. They grasp the political at its very core.

Notes

An earlier version of this chapter appeared in the *American Political Science Review* 84, no. 3 (September 1990). Reprinted by permission of the American Political Science Association.

1. Dryzek and Leonard (1988) contend there is currently a "plethora" of self-analysis within political science, but their listing includes a number of works rather distant from the present discussion of research trends in the United States. Collini et al. (1983), for instance, deal with nineteenth-century British "thinking about politics"; Farr (1988) with Adam Smith and the Scots. In the same line of disciplinary history, but more recent, is Gunnell's (1988) illuminating discussion of the 1940–50 period in U.S. political science; but it too takes a metaperspective on the discipline, rather than the very practical one taken in this essay.

2. The term 'concrete' theory is thus a shortened form of the correct designation, concrete universal theory. While the term 'concrete' has seemed, to some, unnecessarily industrial in tone, it recommends itself by its specificity and has a robustness that makes it easy to remember. Alternatives that might be proposed, such as 'middle-range political theory,' are so diffuse that they fail to provide the sharp definition I believe the method needs if it is to engage attention.

3. The discipline has not wholly failed to recognize individual examples of concrete theory. Niemi (1986, 237) calls attention to the Jacobson and Kernell model, and suggests "we need more of" such theories. Almond (1988, 833) refers to Bates and North, among others, as those who have softened the "hard Right" emphasis on short-run utility maximization through the use of 'sociological' factors. Levi (1987, 685) emphasizes the institutional aspects of Przeworski and Sprague, and of North and Thomas.

4. Kuhn (1962), for instance, tells us everything about paradigms (their origins in scientific socialization, their revolutionary development, the functions they serve in guiding research), but he fails to provide actual examples of just what, in detail, various scientific methodologies include. Popper's (1959) *Logic of Scientific Discovery,* the title of which would suggest interest in the early, theory-

building stages of research, devotes some twenty pages to theory, out of five hundred in the book, and makes only the standard distinctions between 'universal' concepts (such as H_2O, dictator, planet) and 'concrete' ones (such as Napoleon, the Atlantic Ocean). Lakatos (Lakatos and Musgrave 1970) entirely restricts himself to falsification of theories, the negative and positive heuristics that surround them, crucial experiments, and so on. Abraham Kaplan declines to define 'scientific method,' because, among other reasons, he believes there "is no one thing to be defined" (Kaplan 1964, 27). But he does not suggest what the options might be. On the issue of the strictures imposed by the covering law model see Farr (1987), Nelson (1975), and Donagan (1964).

5. Merton's research contains many examples of concrete theorizing. See his discussion of the paradox of relative deprivation (Merton 1957, 227–37). The distinction between middle-range theory and concrete theory is that the former has a wider inclusiveness (across disciplines) while concrete theory and the politics model contain greater internal structure, specifying more clearly within the political science discipline the specific methods appropriate to such inquiry.

6. I do not wish to suggest that situational analysis and concrete theory are by any means equivalent. Situational analysis includes a wide variety of nonpolitical topics (Gombrich on art, for instance), as well as all of microeconomic theory, and Duverger's and Michels's laws (Farr 1987, 56–60). It is undoubtedly premature at present to sort out this diversity into more orderly forms.

7. Because the current essay could not have been kept within manageable limits if citations were given to the full range of literature in each field touched by the concrete theories included here, I concentrate in each case on defining the specific concrete theses, without attempting to provide complete bibliographies. The relevant citations are to be found in each of the original works discussed.

8. A test case for strategic politicians theory occurred in 1982, when, according to the economic model, the Republicans should have lost more congressional seats than they did in the midterm elections. Jacobson and Kernell argue that this unpredicted outcome occurred because the Republican elite deliberately defied the usual nexus between national conditions and party effort, and recruited and trained high-quality candidates as if it were a 'good' year (Jacobson and Kernell 1983, 94–109). This is a strong case for the usefulness of 'process' models in preference to aggregate ones; by describing the actual machinery, they provide more robust explanation than can be given by mere descriptive correlations.

9. In other work, Przeworski (1985) emphasizes substantive questions relating to capitalism rather than method. The fact that many readers will direct attention only to the substantive questions and findings is another argument for bringing out the *methodological* originality here.

10. Skowronek's theory could be brought more nearly into line with the other examples presented here by looking at the broader development of national policy rather than the presidency (see, for instance, Skowronek 1982). However, I believe it to be more interesting to stay with the theory of the presidency and thus to demonstrate the 'reach' of concrete theory into a new area. In addition, Skowronek's larger work (1982) makes points that go beyond the present chapter.

11. Both Kessel and Asher emphasize the point in respect to more unusual presidential candidacies rather than as a general rule. Kessel concludes that "a presidential party at any time is a residue of its past campaigns" and can never

quite go "back to normal" after a Goldwater or a McGovern year (Kessel 1980, 63). Similarly, Asher bases his conclusion on the candidacies of McCarthy and Wallace: "The point is that the behavior of political elites does make a difference in the alternatives available to the electorate and in how the electorate responds to these alternatives. In fact, the very selection of a candidate may introduce issues and concerns into an election that otherwise would not have impinged upon the voter's consciousness" (1984, 221). Neither of these scholars, however, pushes the idea to the level of a general principle, as do Miller and Jennings.

12. A classic work in cognitive psychology possibly throws light on the creation of concrete theories. Bruner, Goodnow, and Austin (1956) distinguished between two methods of problem solving by their experimental subjects. One approach, perhaps the most obvious, was called "simultaneous scanning"; in it, the subject attempted to consider all possible combinations of the problem variables in order to evaluate the hypotheses. This strategy was, the authors noted, highly exacting in memory and deductive capacities. All the other strategies simplified the problem in various ways, either by taking a single hypothesis at a time, or by focusing on single instances and working from that locus toward a solution (Bruner, Goodnow, and Austin 1956, 81–89). The noncomprehensive strategies have an obvious analogy to concrete theorizing. Bruner and his colleagues noted that the focused strategies worked markedly better.

13. Potential areas of further application of concrete methods would include the interplay of decision making among high government officials, leadership and breakdown in revolutionary groups or parties, formal and informal interactions in legislative committees, military–government relations in developing nations, and so on. The theories discussed above also call for greater work on the cognitive description of decision-making elites, especially in respect to their idea systems; this cognitive aspect is particularly central to the work of Skowronek, Miller and Jennings, Przeworski and Sprague, Bates, and George and Smoke.

References

Almond, Gabriel A. 1988. "Separate Tables: Schools and Sects in Political Science." *PS: Political Science and Politics* 21 (fall): 828–42.

Almond, Gabriel A., and James S. Coleman, eds. 1960. *The Politics of the Developing Areas*. Princeton, NJ: Princeton University Press.

Apter, David. 1965. *The Politics of Modernization*. Chicago: University of Chicago Press.

———. 1972. *Ghana in Transition*. Princeton, NJ: Princeton University Press.

Asher, Herbert B. 1984. *Presidential Elections and American Politics*. 3d ed. Homewood, IL: Dorsey Press.

Ball, Terence, ed. 1987. *Idioms of Inquiry: Critique and Renewal in Political Science*. Albany, NY: SUNY Press.

Barber, James David. 1977. *The Presidential Character: Predicting Performance in the White House*. 2d ed. Englewood Cliffs, NJ: Prentice Hall.

———. 1980. *The Pulse of Politics: Electing Presidents in the Media Age*. New York: W. W. Norton.

Barnard, Chester Irving. [1938] 1968. *The Functions of the Executive*. Cambridge, MA: Harvard University Press.

Bates, Robert H. 1981. *Markets and States in Tropical Africa: The Political Basis of Agricultural Policies*. Berkeley: University of California Press.

———. 1983. *Essays on the Political Economy of Rural Africa*. Cambridge: Cambridge University Press.

Bauman, Zygmunt. 1978. *Hermeneutics and Social Science*. New York: Columbia University Press.

Bentley, Arthur F. [1908] 1967. *The Process of Government*. Cambridge, MA: Harvard University Press.

Bienen, Henry, and Nicolas Van de Walle. 1989. "Time and Power in Africa." *American Political Science Review* 83:19–34.

Borger, Robert, and Frank Cioffi, eds. 1970. *Explanation in the Behavioral Sciences*. Cambridge: Cambridge University Press.

Boynton, G. Robert. 1980. *Mathematical Thinking about Politics: An Introduction to Discrete Time Systems*. New York: Longman.

Bruner, Jerome S., Jacqueline J. Goodnow, and George A. Austin. 1956. *A Study of Thinking*. New York: John Wiley.

Buchanan, James M., and Gordon Tullock. [1962] 1965. *The Calculus of Consent*. Ann Arbor: University of Michigan Press.

Campbell, Angus, Philip E. Converse, Warren E. Miller, and Donald E. Stokes. 1964. *The American Voter*. New York: John Wiley and Sons.

———. 1966. *Elections and the Political Order*. New York: John Wiley and Sons.

Chilcote, Ronald H. 1981. *Theories of Comparative Politics: The Search for a Paradigm*. Boulder, CO: Westview Press.

Coleman, James S. 1964. *Introduction to Mathematical Sociology*. New York: The Free Press.

Collini, Stefan, Donald Winch, and John Burrow. 1983. *That Noble Science of Politics: A Study in Nineteenth-Century Intellectual History*. Cambridge: Cambridge University Press.

Cronin, Thomas E. 1980. *The State of the Presidency*. 2d ed. Boston: Little, Brown.

Dahl, Robert A. 1963. *Modern Political Analysis*. Englewood Cliffs, NJ: Prentice Hall.

Dogan, Mattei, and Dominique Pelassy. 1984. *How to Compare Nations: Strategies in Comparative Politics*. Chatham, NJ: Chatham House.

Donagan, Alan. 1964. "Historical Explanation: The Popper-Hempel Theory Reconsidered." *History and Theory* 6:3–26.

Downs, Anthony. 1957. *An Economic Theory of Democracy*. New York: Harper and Row.

Dryzek, John S., and Stephen T. Leonard. 1988. "History and Discipline in Political Science." *American Political Science Review* 82:1245–60.

Easton, David. 1953. *Political System: An Inquiry into the State of Political Science*. New York: Alfred A. Knopf.

———. 1965. *A Systems Analysis of Political Life*. New York: John Wiley and Sons.

Eulau, Heinz. 1963. *The Behavioral Persuasion in Politics*. New York: Random House.

Evans, Peter B., Dietrich Rueschemeyer, and Theda Skocpol, eds. 1985. *Bringing the State Back In*. New York: Cambridge University Press.

Farr, James. 1987. "Resituating Explanation." In Ball 1987, pp. 45–66.

———. 1988. "Political Science and the Enlightenment of Enthusiasm." *American Political Science Review* 82:51–69.

Fenno, Richard F., Jr. 1966. *The Power of the Purse: Appropriations Politics in Congress*. Boston: Little, Brown.

———. 1978. *Home Style*. Boston: Little, Brown.

George, Alexander, and Richard Smoke. 1974. *Deterrence in American Foreign Policy: Theory and Practice*. New York: Columbia University Press.

Glaser, Barney G., and Anselm L. Strauss. 1967. *The Discovery of Grounded Theory: Strategies for Qualitative Research*. Chicago: Aldine.

Gramsci, Antonio. 1971. *Prison Notebooks*. New York: International Publishers.

Gunnell, John G. 1988. "American Political Science, Liberalism, and the Invention of Political Theory." *American Political Science Review* 82:71–87.

Hargrove, Erwin C., and Michael Nelson. 1984. *Presidents, Politics, and Policy*. New York: Alfred A. Knopf.

Harre, Romano. 1970. *The Principles of Scientific Thinking*. Chicago: University of Chicago Press.

———. 1986. *Varieties of Realism: A Rationale for the Natural Sciences*. New York: Basil Blackwell.

Hempel, Carl Gustav. 1965a. "Aspects of Scientific Explanation." In *Aspects of Scientific Explanation and Other Essays in the Philosophy of Science,* by Carl Gustav Hempel, pp. 331–496. New York: The Free Press.

———. 1965b. "The Theoretician's Dilemma: A Study in the Logic of Theory Construction." In *Aspects of Scientific Explanation and Other Essays in the Philosophy of Science*, by Carl Gustav Hempel, pp. 173–226. New York: The Free Press.

Jacobs, Jane. 1970. *The Economy of Cities*. New York: Vintage.

Jacobson, Gary. 1980. *Money in Congressional Elections*. New Haven, CT: Yale University Press.

Jacobson, Gary C., and Samuel Kernell. 1983. *Strategy and Choice in Congressional Elections*. 2d ed. New Haven, CT: Yale University Press.

Janos, Andrew C. 1986. *Politics and Paradigms: Changing Theories of Change in Social Science*. Stanford, CA: Stanford University Press.

Jennings, M. Kent, and Richard G. Niemi. 1981. *Generations and Politics: A Panel Study of Young Adults and Their Parents*. Princeton, NJ: Princeton University Press.

Kahneman, Daniel, Paul Slovic, and Amos Tversky, eds. 1982. *Judgement under Uncertainty: Heuristics and Biases*. Cambridge: Cambridge University Press.

Kaplan, Abraham. 1964. *The Conduct of Inquiry*. San Francisco: Chandler.

Kemeny, John G., and J. Laurie Snell. 1978. *Mathematical Models in the Social Sciences*. Cambridge, MA: MIT Press.

Kernell, Samuel. 1986. *Going Public: New Strategies of Presidential Leadership*. Washington: CQ Press.

Kessel, John H. 1980. *Presidential Campaign Politics*. Homewood, IL: Dorsey Press.

Key, V. O., Jr. 1964. *Politics, Parties, and Pressure Groups.* 5th ed. New York: Thomas V. Crowell.

————. 1966. *The Responsible Electorate: Rationality in Presidential Voting 1936–1960.* Cambridge, MA: Belknap Press.

Kirkpatrick, Jeane J. 1976. *The New Presidential Elite: Men and Women in National Politics.* New York: Russell Sage Foundation and Twentieth Century Fund.

Kramer, Gerald H. 1986. "Political Science as Science." In *Political Science: The Science of Politics,* ed. Herbert F. Weisberg, pp. 11–23. New York: Agathon.

Kuhn, Thomas S. 1962. *The Structure of Scientific Revolutions.* Chicago: University of Chicago Press.

Lakatos, Imre. 1970. "Falsification and the Methodology of Scientific Research Programmes." In *Criticism and the Growth of Knowledge,* ed. Imre Lakatos and Alan Musgrave, pp. 91–196. London: Cambridge University Press.

Lane, Ruth. 1990. "Concrete Theory: An Emerging Political Method." *American Political Science Review* 83, no. 4 (September): 927–40.

Lave, Charles A., and James G. March. 1975. *An Introduction to Models in the Social Sciences.* New York: Harper and Row.

Levi, Margaret. 1987. "Theories of Historical and Institutional Change." *PS: Political Science and Politics* 20:684–88.

Liebenow, J. Gus. 1986. *African Politics: Crises and Challenges.* Bloomington: Indiana University Press.

Lipset, Seymour Martin. 1960. *Political Man: The Social Basis of Politics.* New York: Doubleday Anchor.

Lukacs, Gyorgy. 1971. *History and Class Consciousness.* Cambridge, MA: MIT Press.

Macridis, Roy C. 1955. *The Study of Comparative Government.* New York: Random House.

March, James G., and Johan P. Olsen. 1984. "The New Institutionalism: Organizational Factors in Political Life." *American Political Science Review* 78:734–49.

Meier, Gerald M., and Dudley Seers. 1984. *Pioneers in Development.* Published for the World Bank. New York: Oxford University Press.

Meier, Gerald M., ed. 1987. *Pioneers in Development: Second Series.* New York: Oxford University for the World Bank.

Merton, Robert K. 1957. *Social Theory and Social Structure.* New York: The Free Press.

Miller, Warren E., and M. Kent Jennings. 1986. *Parties in Transition: A Longitudinal Study of Party Elites and Party Supporters.* New York: Russell Sage Foundation.

Nelson, John S. 1975. "Accidents, Laws, and Philosophic Flaws: Behavioral Explanations in Dahl and Dahrendorf." *Comparative Politics* 7:435–57.

Neustadt, Richard E. 1980. *Presidential Power: The Politics of Leadership from FDR to Carter.* 2d ed. New York: John Wiley and Sons.

Niemi, Richard G. 1986. "The Dynamics of Public Opinion." In *Political Science: The Science of Politics,* ed. Herbert F. Weisberg, pp. 225–40. New York: Agathon.

North, Douglass C., and Robert P. Thomas. 1973. *The Rise of the Western World: A New Economic History.* Cambridge: Cambridge University Press.

Olson, Mancur, Jr. 1965. *The Logic of Collective Action.* New York: Schocken.

Parsons, Talcott, and Edward A. Shils, eds. 1951. *Toward a General Theory of Action: Theoretical Foundations for the Social Sciences.* New York: Harper Torchbooks.

Petrocik, John R. 1981. *Party Coalitions: Realignment and the Decline of the New Deal Party System.* Chicago: University of Chicago Press.

Popper, Karl R. 1959. *The Logic of Scientific Discovery.* New York: Harper Torchbooks.

————. 1972. *Objective Knowledge: An Evolutionary Approach.* Oxford: Clarendon Press.

Pressman, Jeffrey L., and Aaron Wildavsky. 1979. *Implementation.* 2d ed. Berkeley: University of California Press.

Przeworski, Adam. 1985. *Capitalism and Social Democracy.* New York: Cambridge University Press.

Przeworski, Adam, and John Sprague. 1986. *Paper Stones: A History of Electoral Socialism.* Chicago: University of Chicago Press.

Pye, Lucien W. 1968. "Description, Analysis, and Sensitivity to Change." In *Political Science and Public Policy,* ed. Austin Ranney, pp. 239–61. Chicago: Markham.

Ricci, David M. 1984. *The Tragedy of Political Science: Scholarship and Democracy.* New Haven, CT: Yale University Press.

Riker, William H. 1962. *The Theory of Political Coalitions.* New Haven, CT: Yale University Press.

Rose, Richard. 1980. *Electoral Participation: A Comparative Analysis.* Beverly Hills, CA: Sage Publications.

Schelling, Thomas. 1963. *Strategy of Conflict.* New York: Oxford Galaxy.

Simon, Herbert A. [1945] 1965. *Administrative Behavior: A Study of Decision-Making Process in Administrative Organization.* New York: The Free Press.

————. 1982. *Models of Bounded Rationality.* Volume Two: Behavioral Economics and Business Organization. Cambridge, MA: MIT Press.

Skowronek, Stephen. 1982. *Building a New American State: The Expansion of National Administrative Capacities 1877–1920.* Cambridge: Cambridge University Press.

————. 1984. "Presidential Leadership in Political Time." In *The Presidency and the Political System,* ed. Michael Nelson, pp. 87–132. Washington, DC: CQ Press.

Stewart, Philip D., Margaret G. Hermann, and Charles F. Hermann. 1989. "Modeling the 1973 Soviet Decision to Support Egypt." *American Political Science Review* 83:35–59.

Stinchcombe, Arthur L. 1968. *Constructing Social Theories.* New York: Harcourt, Brace, World.

Sylvan, Donald A., and Steve Chan, eds. 1984. *Foreign Policy Decision Making.* New York: Praeger.

Tilly, Charles, ed. 1975. *Formation of National States in Western Europe.* Princeton, NJ: Princeton University Press.

Tullock, Gordon. 1965. *The Politics of Bureaucracy.* Washington, DC: Public Affairs Press.

Verba, Sidney. 1985. "Comparative Politics: Where Have We Been, Where Are We Going." In *New Directions in Comparative Politics,* ed. Howard J. Wiarda, pp. 26–38. Boulder, CO: Westview Press.

Wason, Peter Cathcart, and P.N. Johnson-Laird. 1972. *Psychology of Reasoning: Structure and Content.* Cambridge, MA: Harvard University Press.

Watkins, John. 1970. "Imperfect Rationality." In Borger and Cioffi 1970, pp. 167–217.

Wisdom, J. O. 1970. "Situational Individualism and the Emergent Group-Properties." In Borger and Cioffi 1970, pp. 271–96.

3 THE POLITICS MODEL IN POLITICAL RESEARCH

> Whatever it may become in print, in real life politics is vivid in tone and color. Its flavor is in no sense mild and bland, but meaty, savory, salty . . . full of life and action, of dramatic situations and interesting moments.
>
> —Charles E. Merriam (1926, 5)

Metaphors are an important guide for the social sciences, as indeed for all sciences. Adam Smith fixed the idea of 'economics' in the Western mind forever when he pointed out that, rather than depending on the good will of the butcher for one's meat, one had better find out the butcher's needs and enter into exchange with him (Smith 1937). Behavioral psychology, perhaps less happily, invented the metaphor of the T-maze, the trial-and-error box in which innocent white mice were forced to make decisions based on insufficient evidence (Skinner 1953).

Political science has never defined an equivalent metaphor. The classic theorists sought it in what they called the 'state of nature,' where persons were imagined as they might have been before society was established. Hobbes found men tearing one another up, in an embattled world where life was brutal and short; Locke found men mixing their labor with the natural world under the apparently benign rule of natural law; Montesquieu found men quivering in thickets, terrified of one another; Marx saw the strong exploiting the weak; Nietzsche saw the weak exploiting the strong. Given this multiplicity of options, subsequent students of politics have adopted whatever image best fit their preconceptions and have thrown the others out. But the politics model suggests that a more unified metaphor is possible.

Imagine a small American town earlier in the present century. On the outskirts is a fairground where traveling circuses and carnivals periodically visit. Among the personnel of the traveling companies, the town officials, the patrons, and the bystanders, such carnivals may define all the elements present in the political field. There is a main tent where skilled performers walk tightropes, tame lions, and dance in gauze and spangles on the backs of galloping horses.

Spectators pay their money for the temporary excitement of the show, without having anything material to show for it. Outside the main tent are merry-go-rounds and ferris wheels where people pay to be joggled or terrified in controlled safety. Barkers invite passers-by to view unusual or forbidden sights. Prosperous townspeople take their children to enjoy the good clean fun. Other parents leave the family at home and pursue other sorts of fun. In the crowds are pickpockets. Outside the surrounding fence are rogues and thieves. Religious leaders visit to make sure their flocks are not going to the dogs. Town officials post police to curb drunks and ruffians, and to restore lost children to whoever lost them. Strangers collect not to watch the show but the audience. There is music, spectacle, wildness, comedy, occasional tragedy. And in the morning everything is gone.

Keep in mind also the town itself, which serves as a host to these circuses. The town is more stable, more orderly in its government; but it is inextricably a part of the activity at the fairground, for without the town audience and its desire for amusement and profit, the circus would not visit at all. The town interacts with the traveling shows in many ways besides providing customers—by taxing their profits, charging rent for the grounds, prohibiting behavior of which it disapproves, placing safety restrictions on the ferris wheel, posting constables to maintain public order, and so on. The traveling carnivals will also negotiate with the town fathers, seeking concessions, exceptions, and a reasonable right to mislead and fleece the patrons.

The Carnival Becomes Politics

Eventually one of the circuses may stop permanently in the town. As its members become part of the community, a quiet and homogeneous rural village (where not much happened except that the butcher traded with the baker, and everyone went to services on the Sabbath) becomes a political community, full of many different kinds of persons, with many different goals; a community that includes strange and wonderful skills such as rope dancing, and resources such as lions and elephants, or a capacity for deceit.

The simple human relations of the bucolic past turn into sometimes highly dangerous negotiations where people without common experiences or beliefs try to order the town along lines appropriate to their vision of the good society and the good life. People still enjoy a skilled tight-wire act, still enjoy peep shows, still have their pockets picked. But it is no longer a recreational activity. It is government. The politics model meets the analytic needs created by this kind of diverse community.

Even when the politics model is applied to the simplest of human interactions—two people standing and talking at a fork in the road—the whole 'town,' the whole superstructure, is implicitly present because the model sketches out a rich array of political *possibilities* inherent in their interaction. Peter may be attempting to influence Paul to do what Peter wishes him to do. Or the two may be working out an agreement where both combine to influence some third party. If there has been some trouble in the field, they may be devising a response to it. If there is quiet and prosperity, they may be devising ways to cause trouble. Where some set of practices is satisfactory to them, they may be developing defenses against those who might seek change. Where some set of practices is unsatisfactory to them, they may be inventing practices more favorable to their own desires.

When they settle on some course of action, they make it public but often cannot control the outcome, which is determined by what other participants happen to do as they make their own choices. If Peter attacks Stephen, and Stephen simultaneously decides to attack Peter, the outcome will be defined as 'war.' If Peter attacks Stephen and Stephen makes no defense, the outcome is often called 'leadership.' The possible combinations and permutations of these alternatives have been in part worked out by those who have practiced analysis according to the structure of the politics model.

An Expansion of Concrete Theory

The step from concrete theory, devoted to specific topics in political science research, to the more general 'politics' model, which establishes a method of analysis for the larger questions of political science, is short and easy—but not always immediately obvious. Appreciation of the concrete theorists described in the last chapter leads, however, to a growing recognition that not all the examples are as specific as they seem. Policy implementation is a topic not only of interest to students of administration and organizations but is deeply central to all politics. The creation of mass support for political leaders is relevant to interest groups, to political parties, to movements such as socialism, indeed to any political grouping at all. Similarly, challenge and response apply not only in international politics but to every political interaction—from grand issues of war and peace down to minute problems such as parents' attempts to get the kids to bed on time.

In addition to having suspicions that some more general model may be involved in these research examples, a student of political science begins to notice that some writers are working with concrete methods but are going well beyond the limits first defined in Chapter 2. These broader efforts move beyond specific elites and specific policies and take the whole political process as their field of interest. The questions asked by these political scientists are more fundamental, and their approach includes a more extensive inquiry into the basic processes of politics in all the discipline's subfields. This larger scope of political inquiry brings the present discussion to the topic of the 'politics' model.[1]

The Politics Model

A sample of the political science works that represent this general model gives a first view of its scope:[2]

Samuel Huntington (1968) on institutional politics,
Nelson Polsby (1983) on party change,
Terry Moe (1980) on group organization,
Barrington Moore (1966) on transitions to modernity,
Norton Long (1962) on community politics,
Richard Rosecrance (1963) on international political behavior,
Stephen Skowronek (1982) on U.S. national development,
Robert Dahl (1966) on political oppositions, and
Joel Migdal (1988) on the failure of the state.

These writers display great diversity among themselves. They come from various fields within the discipline of political science, from international relations, from American politics, from comparative politics, the study of administration, and from community politics. Their research areas are different, and their findings bear no substantive relation to one another; many of them appear to have no definable 'method' at all. Furthermore, when the discipline classifies the theorists mentioned, it often uses quite different headings: One is a neoinstitutionalist, another is a historian, another eschews theory entirely. But labels may be misleading.

What are the similarities among these works?

1. There is first a vigorous microanalycity that breaks institutional or systemic 'wholes' into component parts such as elites, social or political action groups, mayors, foreign policy decision makers, and so on. Even those whose subject is macroanalytic (such as national development) draw their conclusions from such micro-breakdown of the materials. But the method is not 'reductionist'; individual actors are defined by their institutional and contextual positions, and this bridges the gap between individuals and the wholes of which they are a part.

2. An emphasis on this contextual dimension is a second similarity among these political scientists, their interest in political *processes* in all their rich detail, often focusing on political bargaining and infighting, the "meaty, savory" aspects of politics to which Merriam referred. These processes, furthermore, are seen as dynamically open, tending not to equilibria but to development and change. This aspect provides a needed supplement to more static models.

3. Third and most important, the politics model is recognized by its concern for rounded *explanations* of political events. Explanation is a somewhat slippery concept because what qualifies as an explanation varies with the question being asked, the person making the inquiry, and so on (Hilton 1988; Pitt 1988). But the thrust of the matter is clear enough: One wants "some insight into the structure and *workings of the mechanisms,* above and beyond the capability of predicting and controlling its outcomes" (Railton 1988, 120; emphasis added).

This type of explanation requires a tight, tensile causal chain in which the results of a first interaction change the situation in which the second interaction occurs, and results of the second interaction change the situation in which the third interaction occurs, and so on until the process is, for the defined purposes, complete. The politics model is not, therefore, a disguise for barefoot historicism, with microscopic and indiscriminate description of events. Rather, the data are highly selected, so that the result provides an interconnected explanatory chain that elucidates—as explanation—the logic inherent in the process.[3]

Definition of the Model

The politics model has been defined in Chapter 1 according to ten descriptive points:

- An emphasis on full, contextual political situations
- A focus on individual decision makers
- Attention to individuals' beliefs, values, cognition
- Special attention to the variety of individual goals
- Recognition that interaction among actors is decisive to outcomes
- Inclusion of players' resources—physical, social, personal
- The major role of official and unofficial rules and institutions
- Emphasis on the political process by which values are allocated and the rules and institutions are maintained or changed
- An interactive logic, in which one set of interactions sets the structure for subsequent phases
- Research that plumbs beneath the surface, seeking deeper processes.

Or, in other words, the politics model can be defined as actors of various sorts, defined and constrained by their positions within existing institutions, both formal and informal, interacting with one another on the basis of those roles and the resources identified with them, and in the process of interaction creating, recreating, or replacing the institutional framework within which they act.

The logic of analysis is roughly indicated by a diagram.

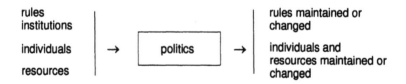

In other words, the analyst begins with the study of individual players who enter the political process with their individual beliefs, goals, and preferences; with the resources held by them, including physical goods and social alliances; and under a set of rules indicating, formally or informally, how some people expect others to behave and how the members define one another's rights and duties.

These individuals, resources, and institutions are brought into contact through the political process, through which goals are evaluated for their compatibility, actions are matched, winners and losers are determined, and status is reevaluated. On the basis of these calculations, the participants enter the next phases. Each time, the ideas and resources of the individuals may have changed, moderately or radically. But each new phase is the 'logical' result of the events that have gone before. To paraphrase Marx, men make and remake their lives, but not always as they wish, nor always as they intend.

As a way of illustrating the strength, the variety, and the analytical characteristics of the politics model, the present chapter discusses a large handful of works in political science. It begins with brief accounts of research in comparative politics by Moore, Dahl, and Migdal, and of research in American politics by Skowronek and Long. More detailed accounts of Rosecrance in international relations and Moe in organization theory give a deeper look into their use of the politics model. Finally, two works, by Huntington and Polsby, are analyzed to bring the 'theory' explicitly to the surface. This is developed in the conclusion to show the type of general result derived from the several examples.

A Theory of Class Interaction

Barrington Moore's study of the processes of modernization (Moore 1966) has always been difficult to classify. The book is both widely read and inadequately understood, admired but rarely replicated. Recognizing the work as an example of the politics model clarifies its contribution to political science. Moore's work is an example of the general paradigm outlined here—actors, resources, goals, processes of interaction, unplanned outcomes—and is of especial interest for the author's willingness to hypothesize actual lines of development.

This achievement is made possible by his use of 'standard' categories to define actors (lord, peasant, bourgeois) and outcomes (democracy, fascism, communism). With these end points settled, Moore is free to devote most of his attention to listing the logical possibilities of each social configuration and to drawing connecting lines from one phase to the next. His achievement can be conceptualized as an extensive game theoretic tree diagram, extending over several centuries of modern history. For each of the political outcomes, a specific route through the chain of possibilities is underlined.

The "fascist syndrome," for instance, requires (1) a strong landed class that either maintains peasant society or creates plantation slavery, (2) and that later allies with the monarchy to increase its repressive support, (3) a weak industrial-commercial class that "throws itself into the arms of the landed aristocracy and the royal bureaucracy, exchanging the right to rule for the right to make money," (4) problems of international competition that lead to increased domestic repression, (5) continued or increased influence of the aristocracy, (6) a forced rationalization of the economy, and (7) "distinguished" political leaders (Moore 1966, 433–40).

Moore is particularly good in his delineation of the 'accidental' factors determining political outcomes. Thus, for instance, the success of peasant revolutions depends not merely on the peasants, but on the presence—not by any means foreordained—of other groups with their own political grievances, which crest at the appropriate time. Absent the right circumstances, peasant revolts come to nothing. So much for the determinists (Moore 1966, 479–80).

The analysis leads to unexpectedly harsh conclusions with respect to industrialization. Modernization, when pursued by moderate means, has created costs "at least as atrocious as those of revolution." Nor does modernization appear to fulfill the desires of 'the people': ". . . there is no evidence that the mass of the population anywhere has wanted an industrial society. . . . all forms of industrialization so far have been revolutions from above, the work of a ruthless minority" (Moore 1966, 505–6).

The Ecology of Community Power

Fans of Norton Long's study of municipal administration, "The Local Community as an Ecology of Games" (1958), will not be surprised to find it classified as an example of the politics model. Long's essay, timeless in its simplicity, clarity, and scope, appeared in that brief period before game theory was captured by the technicians. But its elegance made it a 'hard act to follow' and few took the path it sketched out. Considered in retrospect, in the company of similar general theories, Long's approach can be seen to contain, in a nutshell, all the essential elements of the politics model.

The actors are public and private local groups—municipal departments, state agencies, federal authorities, banks, newspapers, trade unions, chambers of commerce, churches—"occupying a territorial field and interacting with one another." Long gives no ideological weight to the presumption that a territorial system must be unified under a single government ("There need be no Leviathan"). "A great deal of the communities' activities consist of undirected co-operation of particular social structures, each seeking particular goals and, in so doing, meshing with others." "Much of what occurs seems to just happen with accidental trends becoming cumulative over time and producing results intended by nobody" (Long 1958, 140).

Citizens do not participate in the games, according to Long, nor is there any assumption that the players represent citizens. In Long's model the citizens are the 'drama critics' who serve as audience and ultimately as judges of the skill with which the game players perform their roles. (The existence of this audience is what separates natural biological ecologies from political ones; Long 1958, 143). The top political leadership is created by this audience, which expects that leadership will occur; and also by the needs of other elite players for figureheads to finance and legitimate their activities. Often the "power elite," such as the supposedly powerful Cleveland Fifty Club, can hardly be compelled to attend its own meetings. Again and again, in Long's analysis, one notes the way in which adherence to the politics model defeats all ideological or even scientific preconceptions.

A Theory of Institutional Development

A first reading of Stephen Skowronek's microhistory of the politics of state building in the United States in the late nineteenth and early twentieth centuries may lead to the conclusion that it is entirely atheoretical. The book clearly has a thesis—that state building is a less predictable, more raucous affair than political scientists often seem to assume—but no apparent development of theory. While the reader recognizes that there is more to this historical realism than meets the eye, the attempt to 'place' the work within some context in order better to evaluate it has not been an easy one.

Among the present examples of the politics model, the unique qualities of Skowronek's work manifest themselves. There is the distinguishing conceptual framework: actors with mixed goals and resources, engaged in a nearly (but not quite) unpredictable political process or, as Skowronek describes it, an endless "shifting scramble for power and position" (1982, 204). The scope of this shifting scramble is borne out in three histories—of the modernization of the civil service, the army, and business regulation—which directly refute the functionalist thesis of smooth development.

Especially illustrative is Skowronek's history of civil service reform, which contrasts so vividly with the Weberian thesis of bureaucratic rationalization. Rather than being an enlightened movement toward the development of an efficient U.S. government bureaucracy, the rise of the civil service represented a battle with Congress on the part of a new elite seeking to recapture the bases of American political power. Where rhetoric centered on ending the 'abuse' of patronage, Skowronek shows the actual target was the patronage system itself and the party system for which it was the major weapon of control.

The old elite (Congress) wanted to maintain its control; the new elite (professionals arising out of old middle-class groups) wanted to seize control, the federal employees (who became organized only gradually as a result of the battle of the other two players) sought their piece of the pie; and everyone, from presidents to local warlords, played what politics they could while the battle raged. President Grant, for instance, took up reform to deprive his opponents of a political issue against him; the Republican Party reformers, the Halfbreeds, took up the issue against their intraparty rivals, the Stalwarts; outgoing presidents, faced with an incoming president of a different party or faction, swept civil service positions onto the merit list to protect their own supporters from dismissal by the next administration. "The fruits of administrative neutrality (in the civil service system) were thus harvested as an extension of inter-party politics" (Skowronek 1982, 73).

The political process, as Skowronek continually shows, outstripped in speed and ingenuity the reformers who practiced it. As in the equally complex cases of the army and business regulation, civil service reform "followed a logic of its own" which was beyond the control (and frequently the comprehension) of the participants themselves (Skowronek 1982, 75, 178).

A Theory of Opposition Parties

In couching its argument at a rather higher level of abstraction than the other examples of the politics model discussed here, Robert Dahl's *Political Oppositions in Western Democracies* (1966) illustrates an important heuristic: that there may be levels of analysis at which it is excessively difficult, and perhaps unprofitable, to work out the politics model. Dahl's strategy differs from the others discussed here on essentially one point, the definition of the actors. These are reduced to two, governing group and opposition, and the contributors to the Dahl volume provide data on ten cases, eight European nations, the United States, and the United Kingdom.

The complexity of the results and their failure to fit any preconceived analytic scheme led Dahl to depart from the usual custom of providing an introductory framework; instead he attempts to synthesize the individual contributions in several concluding chapters. His framework is typical of other concrete theories included here: "What are the principal characteristics of political oppositions, particularly their goals and strategies," and what are the main "patterns" of politics generated by these oppositions (Dahl 1966, xxi)? Specifically, the analysis focuses on six aspects of oppositions: (1) goals, (2) cohesiveness, (3) competitiveness, (4) distinctiveness, (5) strategies, and (6) the political setting.

The approach, as Dahl notes, is essentially game theoretic, with the exception that it puts emphasis on the parties as strategic actors rather than on the objective characteristics of the contest (Dahl 1966, 336, note 5). Because he must generalize over many countries, Dahl attempts to develop, for each of the six aspects, analytic schemes that define the range of variation in each element. To achieve this, Dahl works out a multidimensional matrix of geometrically increasing proportions—four types of party system by four degrees of competitiveness, by two loci of opposition, by several levels of public support, by several degrees of dispersion of constitutional powers, by several levels of opposition goals, by six opposition strategies. The conclusion is almost foregone: ". . . there is no single prevailing pattern of opposition in Western democracies" (Dahl 1966, 332). Yet the analysis is a powerful one; for a clue to this, one inquires not into party systems but into Dahl's approach itself.

Close study shows that the key factor in Dahl's analysis is his implicit use of the approach of the politics model. Commended at the time for being nonbehaviorist (Lowenstein) and non-'theoretical' (Eckstein), Dahl's synthesis continually reflects sensitivity to the primary requirements of concrete theory: first the description (in specific, empirically applicable terms) of the actors, second the search for patterns of interactive behavior among the actors. This is a striking convergence between Dahl's analysis and the analyses of others who use the politics model.[4]

"Melange" Theory

One of the most recent and most fully developed examples of the politics model is Joel S. Migdal's (1988) *Strong Societies and Weak States,* which deals with the question of why so many Third World nations have failed to develop strong modern state apparatuses, despite the state's pervasive influence on the societies. Migdal designates his approach as a model of "state–society interaction"; the reader gains a more vivid sense of the thrust of the argument with a word Migdal often uses, "melange."

> The image of a melange conveys two facets of the model. First, the groups exercising social control in a society may be heterogeneous both in their form . . . and in the rules they apply. . . . Second, the distribution of social control in society may be among numerous, fairly autonomous groups rather than concentrated largely in the state. (Migdal 1988, 28)

Migdal typically views society not from the top but from the bottom of the social hierarchy. He sees the individual as surrounded "by people with the means to deny others a livelihood" and the means also to provide security and defense. To prosper, or even to survive, the individual must undertake a "careful weighing" of the incentive structures (packages of rewards and sanctions) created by these ambient social organizations. Within this environment, individuals craft "strategies of survival" that allow them to make their way in an uncertain world.

The unexpected aspect of Migdal's approach is that it defines the state as merely one player among the melange of conflicting organizations striving to control society. The battle over "who has the right and ability to make the countless rules that guide people's social behavior" is an open battle, which the state often loses. "Corruption" (a term Migdal avoids using) is not simple malfeasance but represents a fundamental argument over which set of rules is legitimate.

Migdal's approach challenges a surprising array of orthodox theories of politics and the state, both left and right. It denies the linear, upward progression assumed by modernization and development theories; it argues for the importance of the periphery rather than the center; it denies simple Marxist social formations, seeing rather fragmentation; it accepts the importance of international economic conditions but denies that their effect is in any necessary direction; it rejects 'the rediscovery of the state' as Eurocentric and presumptuous; and it objects to any empiricism that concentrates on political elites and fails to recognize systemic and environmental forces (Migdal 1988, xv–xx).

Using materials from Sierra Leone, Israel, Egypt, Mexico, and India, Migdal shows how strong states emerged only in the wake of severe social disruption, often caused by forces outside the society's control, such as colonialism and the world market economy, but also caused from within, as in changes in land tenure and taxation policies (Migdal 1988, 52–72).

The outcome in a particular country is dependent not on a single force but on the interaction of many forces. Where disruption was great but colonial powers kept local power fragmented, the state failed to grow (Sierra Leone). Where disruption was total but centralized organization of indigenous elites was possible, the state became strong (Israel). Where the state was potentially strong, it 'inexplicably' came to destroy itself. Thus in Egypt, Migdal shows, Nasser ruled by balancing the military against the Arab Socialist Union, Nasser's own (and the only recognized) political party. When the military was discredited after the 1967 war, and when the ASU's implementation of Nasser's own reform programs threatened to make it a dominant social force, Nasser chose to give up his reforms rather than support an organization that, by implementing those reforms, could become strong enough to threaten his own position (Migdal 1988, 204–5).

European Concerts as the Politics Model

Richard Rosecrance's study *Action and Reaction in World Politics* (1963) shows that the politics model applies as well to political events beyond national borders as it does to analyses of domestic politics. Students of international affairs may indeed feel they have invented the politics model, but in general this is not so. Realism and neorealism, while focused on political strategy and conflict, have traditionally been highly normative, and not always theoretical in the empirical, testable sense of the term. Rosecrance's work is especially interesting among works by the relatively small number of international systems theorists in its emphasis on historically grounded types of international structure, from the classical eighteenth century, through the several nineteenth-century concerts, to the post–World War II system. He distinguishes his method by the use of the terms "systematic empirical analysis" (1963, 5) or "an empirical model of historical events" (1963, 9), expressing (as does the politics model) the combination of empirical politics and systemic interactions.

Two innovations distinguish Rosecrance's work: a belief in the usefulness of history in the construction of theory, and a belief that international patterns of conflict cannot be seen in isolation but must be understood as "the inadvertent byproduct of domestic change" (Rosecrance 1963, ix–x). Where international actors are viewed usually as nation-states, and the emphasis is on the autonomy of the international system formed by such states, Rosecrance's 'politics' model of international affairs allows for a variety of subnational actors and a far more complex understanding of the levels at which political choice occurs.

The international context of Rosecrance's inquiry leads him to include a factor not explicit in any of the other examples of the politics model tendered here, the "configuration" of actors. The eighteenth-century system was, for instance, composed of a variety of independent actors with similar goals, adequate resources, and predictable inter-actor relations: The result ('if . . . then') of this configuration was that few unmanageable disturbances occurred, demands were for marginal changes only, and stable multipolarity described the system (1963, 232–34). But when one actor changed its behavior in a radical way, the preexisting configuration was changed into another case entirely, despite the persistence of many of the earlier conditions.

The French Revolution changed not only France, but the system. As a result of the changed whole, changes in actor behavior followed. For instance, national loyalties took over where personal loyalties had existed previously; and elites who had before been secure became insecure, with attendant changes in their behavior. The result of elite insecurity, for instance, was that "elites sometimes had to engage in rash actions in foreign relations to cement their internal position," and the "more aggressive personality dispositions" among the elites were drawn forth by the nature of the situation. The revolution and imperium (1789–1814) created new resources, such as the mobilized mass army, and destroyed other resources, such as appeals to traditional legitimacies. Ultimately the system could not cope with its own dynamics, conflict became zero-sum, and the multipolar configuration became one of bipolarity (1963, 236–39).

In terms of the politics model, Rosecrance's study is especially interesting in showing how the individual behaviors of individual actors are aggregated into systemic effects. The 'Napoleon phenomenon,' for instance, might generate research in small groups. Is it true, as Rosecrance's analysis suggests, that particular types of value change in a single member of a group cause complete disintegration of what was until that time an apparently coherent whole?[5] It is particularly interesting, in this light, to compare a theory of international relations with one of interest-group organization.

A General Interest-Group Model

Terry Moe's *The Organization of Interests* (1980) is relevant to the discussion of the politics model for three reasons. First, Moe takes the model into a new area, interest-group politics. Second, of the several examples of the politics model included here, Moe's is the most explicit on the variety of motivations that drive political interactions. Third, Moe locates his work in another theoretical tradition, rational-choice theory modified as the new institutionalism, as does another work that I believe falls within the politics model (Kiser and Ostrom 1982), and this provides a useful point for contrasting the approaches.

The thrust of Moe's interest-group model is of wider consequence than a simple focus on interest-group behavior would imply, for it inquires into the ways in which leadership emerges out of an apparently undifferentiated mass. Beginning with Olson's model of interest-group membership choices (1968), Moe takes a larger organizational approach by introducing the 'entrepreneur' who seeks followers by offering a benefits package that can only be devised by an aspiring leader who intuitively understands the deep, perhaps unexpressed, desires and needs of some social grouping (1980, 36–40). This entrepreneur is more than the leader of a preorganized group. In Moe's treatment he becomes comparable to a king, a revolutionary, or a charismatic leader—all examples in varying ways of important questions of leadership behavior.

Moe emphasizes this political aspect of interest-group behavior by including, along with the entrepreneurs, 'rival' entrepreneurs, who by their very presence turn a tidy organizational model into a rampantly political one. Moe's other major innovation is to include explicitly a whole range of social and political motivations that may direct any of the players: friendship, status, principles—as well as economic self-interest (1980, 113–17).[6] Adding actors outside the organization who may control values that the entrepreneur wants to offer members, and staff who may be at cross-purposes with the leadership, Moe's model takes on the 'politics' emphasis typical of the model as it has been described in the present essay; and becomes formally equivalent, say, to Huntington's analysis of whole societies in the same terms, or Rosecrance's analysis of how international actors create order in international systems.

Moe's theory, located within this framework, shows the scope of the politics model. The theory has six elements: (1) Individuals are not permanently stratified in group roles, such as leader and follower, but may move about; their bargaining positions are the dynamic result of the organizational situation, which for external reasons may come to favor new leaders over the old. (2) This dynamism is constrained by a tendency toward "solidification" of patterns (compare Huntington's institutionalization). (3) Larger members benefit disproportionately because they have more resources to constrain the incentives of other players. (4) Smaller members may attempt to create subgroups (compare Polsby's factions) but this in itself will not equalize their strength. (5) Staff are not neutral and may use their positional advantages to shape outcomes. (6) Alliances with outside groups may be crucial to any player's success (1980, 110–11).

Moe comments that the inclusion of nonmaterial incentives "dramatically enlarges the scope of the analysis" in comparison to economic models (1980, 112). But I would like to suggest that the breadth of incentives effectively *removes* Moe's theory from an economic realm. Both Moe, more recently (1987), and Ostrom (1991) have worked toward an integration of, or complementarity between, rational-choice theory and institutional analysis.

It would be premature to try to settle such a question now; obviously the politics model's emphasis on decisional logic links it to economic-choice theory, and its emphasis on institution building links it to the new institutionalism (March and Olsen 1984). Our study of the politics model suggests, however, that one need not go to other disciplines in search of theoretical cutting edges, but that there is, in the politics model, an indigenous tradition already available—one that may prove a more flexible method than those derived from economics, and equally effective in respect to political phenomena.

The Politics of Development

Samuel Huntington's *Political Order in Changing Societies* (1968) is an appropriate work with which to develop the inquiry into the politics model because the work is so widely known, and because it is characteristic in several ways of both the strengths and weaknesses of the approach. The book disguises its theoretic qualities extremely well: It begins with no introductory discussion of theory, no claim to be building theory, no 'methodological preface.' Instead Huntington begins immediately with questions of substance—the nature of political development and modernization and the means for realizing them; the search for political community, and the means for achieving institutionalization (1968, 8–13).

This apparently pure 'macro' level approach is heightened by a well-known set of macroconclusions: the problems of violence, the need for forceful organization to create sufficient power to maintain national stability, the danger of national decay. But despite much that was traditional in Huntington's analysis, his conclusions were atypical of the development writings of the period, many of which assumed a linear 'progress' from old to new societies (Almond and Coleman 1960; Almond and Verba 1963; Lipset 1959; Riggs 1964; Rostow 1963).[7] Atypical conclusions (what more formal theorists call counterintuitive hypotheses) are one rule of thumb for recognizing cases in which theoretical activity may be present even if it is not announced.

Huntington's own definition of his work is a general theory of institutionalization, which he defines as "the process by which organizations and procedures acquire value and stability," the result of differences between, and therefore conflict among, different social groups (Huntington 1968, 12, 11). Huntington's description of his 'naked' social process can be seen in retrospect as a clear statement of the 'politics' model.

> In all societies specialized social groups engage in politics. What makes such groups seem more "politicized" in a praetorian society is the absence of effective political institutions capable of mediating, refining,

and moderating group political action. In a praetorian system forces confront one another nakedly; . . . Each group employs means which reflect its peculiar nature and capabilities. The wealthy bribe; students riot; workers strike; mobs demonstrate; and the military coup. (Huntington 1968, 196)

That the quotation defines the core of a dynamic interactive model is somewhat obscured by calling it a "praetorian system," since the narrower definition of that term, the intervention of the military in politics, has been better remembered than the broader definition, which is the more important in the present context. It is the broader definition—praetorianism as the more or less naked confrontation of various groups in society—that guides Huntington's subsequent analysis.

This analysis falls into two major branches: first, how does a traditional monarch or leader personally attempt to modernize the nation; and second, how does a nation 'modernize itself' through the political interaction of its component groups. The first question, how a leader might direct the modernization processes, is answered in a way that is partly 'advice to princes' and partly anticipates 'postdevelopment' writers (Bates 1981 and North and Thomas 1973), who see development as a practical political process rather than as system-level aggregate change.

A Theory of Politics

To illustrate its logical interconnectedness, a part of Huntington's argument may be rewritten more formally.

> *Axiomatic assumptions:* Actors include both individuals (here the leader) and groups (here the social interests).
> *Postulates:* At time 't' the groups will be religious authorities, landowners, military, etc. At time 't + 1' the groups will also include intelligentsia, bourgeoisie, urban workers, peasants.
> *Axiomatic assumption:* Each actor has different goals.
> *Postulates:* The leader's goal is to stay in office and to modernize, lest failure to do so should cause discontent (1968, 155); religious authorities' aims vary according to whether the church is or is not independently wealthy; aristocrats' goals are protection of their own interests against the king, an interest that motivates them to espouse republican government (1968, 160).

General conclusion: The outcome depends on how many resources each actor has, and the alliances it is able to make with other actors.

Hypothesis: If a modernizing opposition has a religious tradition that can rally the masses against the leader, then it will probably be able to overthrow that leader (1968, 161).

Hypothesis: If a modernizing monarch can blend enough 'new' people into the bureaucracy to gain its adherence without alienating the aristocracy, then the monarch will undercut the influence of that aristocracy, and perhaps succeed temporarily (1968, 162–63).

The remainder of Huntington's chapter piles hypothesis upon hypothesis as he works out the various combinations and permutations of the assumptions and conditions he laid down at the beginning. For our purpose here—evaluating Huntington's 'theoretical' quality—it is interesting to note how he constantly cycles between presenting his hypotheses and testing them. Huntington does not simply give examples, as an historian might do; he 'controls' for variables, albeit unobtrusively, and tests his hypothesized correlations. Two "traditional societies of similar size, similar geography, similar economies, and similar ethnic make-up" are compared, for instance, to see if their major difference, the distribution of political power, affects the dependent variable, the level of socioeconomic change (1968, 171).

Huntington's discussion of praetorianism, in its broad definition denoting societies where groups confront one another without institutional structures, is part of the inquiry into how societies may, under some circumstances, modernize themselves. He begins by defining three forms of praetorianism, depending on which groups are present—the landowners, clergy, and military in the 'oligarchical' form; students and lower-echelon military in the 'radical' form, and so on (1968, 199, 204, 210). Huntington then, having defined the types of actors that will be present in different cases, again works out the permutations, which depend on the type of goals held by each group. The range of these goals goes considerably beyond those goals postulated, say, in an economic model; they may include "efficiency, honesty, and national loyalty" as well as the narrower forms of self-interest (1968, 203). Once again here as well, Huntington is lavish with his 'if . . . then' hypotheses: If labor faces the allied political and military forces, then it loses; if the army joins labor groups, the government will fall, etc. (1968, 214, 215).

From these basic hypotheses Huntington derives aggregate regularities. When no alliances occur, "praetorianism feeds on itself" as direct action by one group encourages direct action by other groups, reinforcing the power of independent groups "at the expense of political authority" (1968, 215). In the extreme case, a seizure of power from the government "represents the end of a political struggle and the recording of its results, *just as it takes place on election day* in a democratic country" (1968, 219; emphasis added).

I do not wish to suggest, of course, that one must agree with Huntington's analysis. My point is more technical: that despite generations of readers who have looked only at Huntington's conclusions and have thought those conclusions were derived more from opinion than from any theory, in fact Huntington's whole line of approach is rigorously theoretical. It begins with axioms, includes postulates, empirical generalizations, and hypotheses, and puts these together in a coherent logical whole. In these ways, it exemplifies the politics model as defined in the present essay.

Reform of a Political Party System

On the surface it might seem that nothing could be further from any kind of theoretical commitment than Nelson Polsby's study of reform in the U.S. party system, *The Consequences of Party Reform* (1983). Polsby himself elsewhere insists he is a 'fox' rather than a 'hedgehog,' suggesting he would not touch a theory with a ten-foot pole (Baer, Jewell, and Sigelman 1991, 175). Yet such a judgment seems rather to reflect what has been called the 'invisibility' of the politics model, and it seriously underestimates the depth and originality of the analytic method underlying the political details of Polsby's work. The argument is compact: ". . . changing the rules of politics changes the incentives for political actors; . . . changing incentives leads to changes in political behavior; . . . changing behavior changes political institutions and their significance . . ." (Polsby 1983, 5).

Polsby's conceptual approach focuses first on 'systemic' factors in American government, not single institutions but the interactions of institutions with one another, "tracing out how changes in one part of the system affect changes in others" (1983, xii). Second, he focuses on individual choices, "a series of explicit choices by politicians" that create political effects for the system (1983, 4). That this approach is theoretical is shown by Polsby's emphasis on his 'arrangement' of the facts, not simply the facts themselves: He calls this a "line of argument." In effect it is the microanalytic logical analysis characteristic of what is here called the politics model. Other arrangements of the facts are possible, Polsby says, and he invites the reader to present such alternatives, to engage in a debate over a model-based explanatory theory.[8] Such writing is a long way from mere description of events.

Still focusing on individual choices by candidates and politicians, Polsby moves to a broader analysis of the sociopolitical situation each faces. Polsby defines the basic element of political interaction, classically, as factions: groups based on "natural bedrock interests." Coalitions are less fundamental, and the problem for reformers is how to create alliances that will keep politicians' "inherent antipathy" for one another from splintering the political system (1983, 66; the comparison here with "praetorianism" is obvious). The 'rules' of the system are what control behavior by presenting incentives to individual actors, and in the present instance 'majority rule' provides the incentive to engage in coalition behavior. Primary elections, which either are, or are viewed by the press as, plurality contests, where votes count even if a candidate does not come in first, discourage coalition building (1983, 66–67).

A 'Democratic' Theory

What interests Polsby, in addition to his criticism of the reforms themselves, is the 'logic' of this process. A 'change in the rules' changes the decision environment, and individual actors change their strategies in response. Because the rule changes studied here were relatively minor (as compared, say, with a convention changing a nation's constitution) and because the changes were highly focused (on a single party, although some reforms spread to both parties), Polsby provides a cameo example of the exact way in which rules are connected to individual behavior in a social context. The logic of Polsby's explanatory sequences raises them to the level of theory (1983, 53–64).

> *Postulate:* That the rules are changed, centralizing control of the party's election of its primary delegates.
> *Hypothesis:* No longer in control of the process, state leaders will be uncertain as to what selection method will pass muster at the national convention level.

Hypothesis: When in doubt, decision makers in a given cultural milieu will choose a method that is difficult to criticize.

Empirical generalization: 'Democratic' procedures, including primary elections, are largely invulnerable to criticism in the United States.

Conclusion: State party leaders will adopt the method of primary elections to choose presidential delegates (1983, 56).

When this syllogism has been worked out, Polsby then evaluates the conclusion for secondary effects.

Premise: If we hold primaries, the state will get media attention.

Fact: Media attention is desirable.

Conclusion: Primaries are, for this additional reason, a good choice.

Similar arguments follow for other premises: 'If we hold primaries, candidates will come and spend money; money is desirable; therefore . . .' (1983, 57). Polsby's theory about the connection among the rules, the incentives, the individual decision makers, and the system as a whole shows the characteristics central to the politics model, emphasizing the logical interconnections of individuals and the rules the participants make, sometimes without full appreciation of the consequences, to govern themselves.

A Summary Model

The politics model has been laid out, in this chapter, in a way designed to emphasize the diversity of the types of politics that it has demonstrated its capacity to explain. It is therefore helpful to reemphasize the common model at the core of these different types of research.

Actors use their resources (physical, cognitive, and structural) in the attempt to realize their goals (preferred states of affairs) through the imposition, upon the arena as a whole, of rule sets that effect their goals. These rule sets redefine the sociopolitical structures and the actors' goals and resources.

On the surface, this postulate looks like an old-fashioned decision model, but the comparison is inadequate because of the scope and richness of the contextual factors within which the politics model places the actors. This context includes cognitive skills, social roles, cultural norms and patterns, and the strategic opportunities offered by the size and nature of the opposition.

The politics model can be summarized further in terms of a dynamic algorithm that reveals its inner dynamic, the expression of the 'process' upon which scientific realism places such explanatory emphasis.

1. Each actor, within a context formed by its cognitive and resource capabilities, evaluates its goals and opportunities and decides to conform or fight (George and Smoke 1974; Huntington 1968; Moe 1980; Moore 1966).
   Definition: Conform means to accept the opportunities offered by the mix of actor resources and opportunities, and to take the more desirable, or less painful, option (Dahl 1966; Long 1962).
   Definition: Fight means to reject the conventional alternatives and to strive for political precedence, including the right to remake the rules (Migdal 1988; Pressman and Wildavsky 1979).
2. Where all conform (to existing institutions), the system remains structurally stable (Dahl 1966; Long 1962; Rosecrance 1963).
3. Where one decides to fight and the rest conform, the fighter wins (Huntington 1968; Kaplan 1964; Moe 1980).
4. Where at least two decide to fight, the several types of resources (including alliances) are sequentially matched through the political process, and the 'stronger' wins (Migdal 1988; Moore 1966; Skowronek 1982).
5. Winners, within their existing cognitive capacities, remake the rules in what they think is their own interest, redefining resources, allocations, and institutions (Dahl 1966; Kiser and Ostrom 1982; Migdal 1988; Polsby 1983; Rosecrance 1963).
6. Continue this loop (points 1–5) as the 'politics' process develops.

Conclusion

> Just as some plants bear fruit only if they don't shoot up too high, so . . . the leaves and flowers of theory must be pruned and the plant kept close to its proper soil—experience.
> —Clausewitz On War (Paret 1986, 198)

Political scientists, for reasons best left to future historians of the discipline to uncover, have often tended to prefer theories from outside the discipline to theories that are homespun. At various times, political scientists have sought to enrich the discipline with sociological theories (e.g., Parsons 1951) or anthropological concepts (as with Almond and Coleman 1960), or economic theory (Downs 1957). Political theorists have also set aside their own theoretic traditions as a special field without direct impact on political research (Gunnell 1986). Many political scientists have sought deliberately to remove themselves from daily politics, either in the service of professionalism (Ricci 1984), the service of government (Seidelman 1985), or of methodological rigor itself (Easton 1953). Thus, when an indigenous political model sprouts without any real attention from the discipline, and continues to grow over the years, it may be discounted as being 'mere' politics. This seems an unnecessary waste of resources.

The politics model has had a long history in political science, but it has often been the history of an ugly duckling who seems out of place among its siblings and only much later—if it survives at all—turns into a swan. The underlying message of the works discussed here is that political science does best when it follows its own instincts, trusts in its own intimate knowledge of its own particular materials, and does not give itself over to philosophers more concerned with conceptual order than scientific creativity. Along with the other approaches now participating usefully in the political science discipline, it seems reasonable to admit the politics model, which has shown itself to be a solid and useful citizen.

The politics model described here appears, by the quality of its practitioners and their research results, to represent an unobtrusive breakthrough in the conduct of political inquiry. Still in question is the willingness of political scientists to accept a new type of theory, a theory that is integral to the phenomena described. Yet the economists were willing to base their theoretical models on something as everyday as the English shopkeeper. Political scientists may find that a similar strategy is effective.

Notes

1. Alternative names for the approach suggested themselves, but were for one or another reason unsuitable. In one sense it might be called a political behavior model, but this term carries too many imprecise meanings (Dahl 1961a). In another sense it might be seen as a power model, except that the power school has

been buried so effectively as to be beyond recall (March 1966). Political groups also have a strong role in the model, but the term 'group' too would be misleading because of the strong normative associations in group theory (Garson 1974, 1518–19). Political 'process' is another possible solution, but the term lacks precision. Finally, therefore, the simplest term seems to be the best. The use of the term 'politics' rather than the normal adjectival form, 'political,' is designed to avoid charges of imperialism. Calling the model a political model would suggest claims to universality. The term 'politics' avoids such claims while serving also to focus attention on the model's concern with nuts-and-bolts politics. I have resisted the temptation to call it the sausage model, which seems unduly cheerful; although the garbage can model provided some precedent (Cohen, March, and Olsen 1972).

2. The argument applies only to the works to which specific citations are given; many of the authors included here have published numerous works, not all of which demonstrate the politics model. It is well to reiterate here the degree to which concrete theory does not fit into the usual categories. It is quite distinct from the models of macrolevel theorists who deal only with whole-system phenomena such as 'demands and supports,' 'adaptation, integration, boundary maintenance,' or 'penetration, distribution, the imperatives of equality' (Binder 1971; Easton 1965; Parsons 1951). The politics model is equally distinct from behavioral approaches. Recently Lowi has argued that the behavioralists particularly ignored "the political game" and "politics in the vulgar sense" (Lowi 1992, 3); this is just what the politics model emphasizes. Similarly Seidelman and Harpham associate behavioralism with the 'third tradition' of state building and liberalism, neither of which holds an important place in the politics model (Seidelman and Harpham 1985, 8–10). Ricci further notes behavioralism's emphasis on method (Ricci 1984, 140); but the politics model makes no overt methodological efforts. So the politics model is not behavioral in the standard senses. A third possible classification for the politics model might be in institutionalism, neoinstitutionalism, or various forms of rational-choice theory. But this alternative fails also, because institutionalism is either macroanalytic (Steinmo et al. 1992), or methodologically sophisticated (March and Olson 1984), and the politics model is neither. The discussion in Chapter 6 clarifies these issues.

3. That the model is not simply equivalent to any work that contains detailed political description is shown in the two 'negative cases' discussed in Chapter 4, which includes analysis that is extremely sophisticated in historical and conceptual terms but does not manifest the characteristics required of the theoretical approach here described.

4. Compare the politics model with Dahl's conclusion to the well-known *Who Governs* (1961b, 315–24). The thrust of his analysis is that the "American Creed" forces citizens (especially ethnic groups) to trust the politicians to govern. Given this tolerance, elite politics goes on above the heads of the people, with leaders' primary concern being to maintain their place in the status quo. Only when an elite group thinks it cannot succeed otherwise will it appeal to the people. The actors in the final battle are the 'legitimists' and the 'dissenters' (1961b, 321–24). This reduction and formalization of a complex political situation shows all the marks of the politics model as defined here.

5. A particularly interesting example of the use of the politics model in inter-

national relations is a paper by Ferguson and Mansbach that deconstructs international systems to inquire into the evolution of international society. The authors make the vital point that "at any given point in time, there exist side by side numerous potential and actual political forms," and each individual is connected by various crosscutting loyalties to different political objects (1992, 6).

6. This of course rediscovers Lasswell, thereby reemphasizing the continued relevance of certain central concerns for those implicitly using the politics model. See the discussion of Key and Lasswell in Chapter 4.

7. Almond, in a recent survey, redefines Huntington's work more closely within the mainstream, but this seems primarily a result of the new interest in the state, an interest that did not exist in the earlier period (Almond in Weiner and Huntington 1987, e.g., 439–40).

8. That the work is not simply history is suggested by Polsby himself, who apologizes for the results of his analysis (1983, 5), saying they probably are not what people expected. This suggests that the very logic of the analysis may have carried the study further than its author foresaw.

References

Almond, Gabriel A., and James S. Coleman, eds. 1960. *The Politics of the Developing Areas.* Princeton, NJ: Princeton University Press.

Almond, Gabriel A., and Sidney Verba. 1963. *The Civic Culture.* Princeton, NJ: Princeton University Press.

Baer, Michael A., Malcolm E. Jewell, and Lee Sigelman, eds. 1991. *Political Science in America: Oral Histories of a Discipline.* Lexington: University Press of Kentucky.

Bates, Robert H. 1981. *Markets and States in Tropical Africa: The Political Basis of Agricultural Policies.* Berkeley: University of California Press.

Binder, Leonard, James S. Coleman, Joseph LaPalombara, Lucien W. Pye, Sidney Verba, and Myron Weiner. 1971. *Crisis and Sequences in Political Development.* Princeton, NJ: Princeton University Press.

Cohen, Michael, James March, and Johan Olsen. 1972. "A Garbage Can Model of Organizational Choice." *Administrative Science Quarterly* 17 (March): 1–25.

Dahl, Robert A. 1961a. "The Behavioral Approach in Political Science: Epitaph for a Monument to a Successful Protest." *American Political Science Review* 55:763–72.

———. 1961b. *Who Governs.* New Haven, CT: Yale University Press.

———, ed. 1966. *Political Oppositions in Western Democracies.* New Haven, CT: Yale University Press.

Downs, Anthony. 1957. *An Economic Theory of Democracy.* New York: Harper and Row.

Easton, David. [1953] 1964. *The Political System: An Inquiry into the State of Political Science.* Chicago: University of Chicago Press.

———. 1965. *A Systems Analysis of Political Life.* New York: John Wiley and Sons.

———. 1990. *The Analysis of Political Structure.* New York: Routledge.

Ferguson, Yales H., and Richard W. Mansbach. 1992. "Multiple Actors and the

Evolution of International Society." Presented at the annual meeting of the American Political Science Association (September).

Garson, G. David. 1974. "On the Origins of Interest-Group Theory." *American Political Science Review* 68, no. 4 (December): 1505–19.

George, Alexander, and Richard Smoke. 1974. *Deterrence in American Foreign Policy: Theory and Practice.* New York: Columbia University Press.

Gunnell, John G. 1986. *Between Philosophy and Politics: The Alienation of Political Theory.* Amherst: University of Massachusetts Press.

Hilton, Denis J., ed. 1988. *Contemporary Science and Natural Explanation: Commonsense Conceptions of Causality.* New York: New York University Press.

Huntington, Samuel P. 1968. *Political Order in Changing Societies.* New Haven, CT: Yale University Press.

Kaplan, Abraham. 1964. *The Conduct of Inquiry.* San Francisco: Chandler.

Kiser, Larry L., and Elinor Ostrom. 1982. "A Metatheoretical Synthesis of Institutional Approaches." In *Strategies of Political Inquiry,* ed. Elinor Ostrom, pp. 179–220. Beverly Hills, CA: Sage Publications.

Lipset, Seymour Martin. 1959. *Political Man: The Social Basis of Politics.* New York: Doubleday Anchor.

Long, Norton E. [1958] 1962. "The Local Community as an Ecology of Games." In *The Polity,* Chicago: Rand McNally. Originally published in the *American Journal of Sociology* 44 (November 1958): 251–61.

Lowi, Theodore J. 1992. "The State in Political Science: How We Became What We Study." *American Political Science Review* 86, no. 1 (March): 1–7.

March, James G. 1966. "The Power of Power." In *Varieties of Political Theory,* ed. David Easton, pp. 39–70. Englewood Cliffs, NJ: Prentice Hall.

March, James G., and Johan P. Olsen. 1984. "The New Institutionalism: Organizational Factors in Political Life." *American Political Science Review* 78, no. 3 (September): 734–49.

Merriam, Charles E. 1926. "Progress in Political Research." *American Political Science Review* 20, no. 1 (February): 1–13.

Migdal, Joel S. 1988. *Strong Societies and Weak States: State–Society Relations and State Capabilities in the Third World.* Princeton, NJ: Princeton University Press.

Moe, Terry M. 1980. *The Organization of Interests: Incentives and the Internal Dynamics of Political Interest Groups.* Chicago: University of Chicago Press.

———. 1987. "Interests, Institutions, and Positive Theory: The Politics of the NLRB." In *Studies of American Political Development,* ed. Karen Orren and Stephen Skowronek, vol. 2, pp. 236–99.

Moore, Barrington, Jr. 1966. *The Social Origins of Dictatorship and Democracy.* Boston: Beacon Press.

North, Douglass C., and Robert P. Thomas. 1973. *The Rise of the Western World: A New Economic History.* Cambridge: Cambridge University Press.

Olson, Mancur, Jr. 1968. *The Logic of Collective Action.* New York: Schocken.

Ostrom, Elinor. 1991. "Rational Choice Theory and Institutional Analysis: Toward Complementarity." *American Political Science Review* 85, no. 1 (March): 237–43.

Paret, Peter, ed. 1986. *Makers of Modern Strategy: From Machiavelli to the Nuclear Age.* Princeton, NJ: Princeton University Press.

Parsons, Talcott. 1951. *The Social System.* New York: The Free Press of Glencoe.
Pitt, Joseph C., ed. 1988. *Theories of Explanation.* New York: Oxford University Press.
Polsby, Nelson W. 1983. *Consequences of Party Reform.* New York: Oxford University Press.
Pressman, Jeffrey L., and Aaron Wildavsky. 1979. *Implementation.* 2d ed. Berkeley: University of California Press.
Railton, Peter. 1988. "A Deductive-nomological Model of Probabilistic Explanation." In Pitt 1988.
Ricci, David M. 1984. *The Tragedy of Political Science: Scholarship and Democracy.* New Haven, CT: Yale University Press.
Riggs, Fred W. 1964. *Administration in Developing Countries.* Boston: Houghton Mifflin.
Rosecrance, Richard N. 1963. *Action and Reaction in World Politics: International Systems in Perspective.* Westport, CT: Greenwood.
Rostow, Walt W. 1960. *The Stages of Economic Growth.* New York: Cambridge University Press.
Seidelman, Raymond, with Edward J. Harpham. 1985. *Disenchanted Realists: Political Science and the American Crisis 1884–1984.* Albany, NY: SUNY Press 1985. With a rejoinder by Skocpol, pp. 86–96.
Skinner, B. F. 1953. *Science and Human Behavior.* New York: The Free Press.
Skowronek, Stephen. 1982. *Building a New American State: The Expansion of National Administrative Capacities 1877–1920.* Cambridge: Cambridge University Press.
Smith, Adam. [1776] 1937. *An Inquiry into the Nature and Causes of the Wealth of Nations.* New York: Modern Library.
Steinmo, Sven, Kathleen Thelen, and Frank Longstreth, eds. 1992. *Structuring Politics: Historical Institutionalism in Comparative Analysis.* Cambridge: Cambridge University Press.
Weiner, Myron, and Samuel P. Huntington, eds. 1987. *Understanding Political Development.* Boston: Little, Brown.

4 DISTINGUISHING AND CONSTRUCTING POLITICS MODELS

Legend has it that once upon a time, in the not too distant past, a panel of distinguished political scientists was convened and asked to decide upon the crucially important issue of when the discipline of political science should be considered to have begun. Was it long ago with Socrates and Plato? Or did it begin with thinkers of the Renaissance, such as Machiavelli? Perhaps John Locke should have pride of place? Or John Stuart Mill? Or perhaps the political science discipline should not be considered to have begun until the present century, when some defining figure such as Charles Merriam at the University of Chicago attempted to chart a new course for all the modern social sciences. The issue was thought to be important because knowing the nature of the founding father might shed some light on the nature of the discipline. The panel of political scientists thus met and debated, while interested spectators waited in some suspense for the results.

When the ballots were opened, their contents did indeed shed light on the nature of political science. All but one of the panel members had designated as the starting point of the political science discipline the day he himself had received his doctoral degree. Initially this quite egocentric result was thought to be a disappointment, but wiser heads among the audience consulted and agreed that although the answer had not been exactly what anyone expected, the principle it expressed was very nearly accurate: Political scientists are wont to place a very high importance on their own immediate time period, and they have a cavalier confidence that nothing in the previous history of the political science discipline is likely to be at all helpful to their theories or their research.[1]

A particularly fierce example of this tendency to throw out its past was the political science discipline's widespread agreement in the early years of the behavioral revolution to discard several centuries of politi-

cal theory and to start out 'fresh,' casting to the winds whole generations of analytic political theory on the grounds that it was unaccept-
ably normative (Gunnell 1986).[2]

An Openness to the Past

Such an attitude is shortsighted. At best, it weakens the weight of
political research by depriving it of explicit roots in classical political
questions. At worst, it wastes the time of scholars as they must continually reinvent ideas, methods, and approaches that might have been
readily available had they had a living history to bring them to contemporary attention. Even people without any particular affection for the
glories of history might agree that a friendlier relationship with the past
would better serve political science's progress.

The first purpose of the present chapter, therefore, is to look
backward in time, both to identify and to acknowledge cases in
which the politics model has been used by political thinkers of the
classical past (Plato), the 'modern' past (Machiavelli), and the more
recent past (Harold Lasswell and V. O. Key Jr.). Related to this
recognition of political scientists from the past who have used the
concrete model in their inquiries is the identification within the existing body of current political research of studies that provide all
the raw materials for the construction of politics models but do not
themselves take the final step. The present chapter shows how secondary analysis can use such materials in constructing formalized
models of political idea systems, using a classic work in political
culture.

Finally there is the question of how to draw limits around the politics model. This issue has earlier been joined in the discussion of the
ways in which the politics model goes beyond traditional behavioralism, but needs to be expanded to make clear that mere richness in
concrete data or in conceptual analysis does not by itself make research
an example of the politics model. Two research studies are analyzed
from this perspective. While both are excellent, the analysis
demonstrates in detail why neither, despite some apparent similarities,
fits the politics model. This analysis shows that the politics model is a
distinctive method, not equivalent merely to "good writing about politics" in general, but imposing strong requirements of dynamic analysis
and explanation on those who employ it.

Debts to the Past, Present, and Future

The first section of this chapter starts with a very early example of the use of the politics model, suggesting that when Plato dealt with 'imperfect' societies (rather than the perfect Republic), he shifted gears. Instead of dealing with grand universal truths, in this case, Plato showed how human behavior is constrained by the interplay between personal goals and the surrounding environment, and how the behavior of one generation is subject to criticism and transformation by subsequent generations. Plato's approach is process oriented and dynamic, and emphasizes explanation as a function of close attention to the nuts and bolts of social interaction. All this makes it a fine example of the politics model.

Discussion then moves to Machiavelli, for whom the politics model was not an occasional pastime, as it was for Plato, but represented the whole of his political theory. Machiavelli, with his constant sharp cutting away of all surface illusions to reveal the harsh internal mechanisms of political interaction, stands indeed as the father of the politics model.

The inquiry into the sources and exemplars of the politics model then turns to two well-known political scientists from this century who bridged the period between 'traditional' and 'behavioral' approaches to politics, V. O. Key Jr. and Harold Lasswell. Both are seen to have based essential parts of their theoretical work on analytic frameworks that can be best understood as examples of the politics approach defined here.

Another Footnote to Plato

Students of politics often think it is tiresome to trace everything back to Plato. Such a procedure smells dusty and pedantic; anything that happened so far back must surely be irrelevant to the concerns of the present! The problem with Plato is, however, that he chastens all who think the old-timers must be old-fashioned. The mark of the true classic is that it never becomes dated—its insights stand sufficiently outside time that their relevance remains vivid centuries later. So going back to original sources is not pedantic but useful.[3]

Here the concern is with Book Nine of Plato's *Republic,* the section that discusses, in a thoroughly concrete way, what brings down the perfect political system described in the rest of the book, a political system guided by the wise, protected by the brave, and made prosperous by the greedy. Plato's description of the decline in political rectitude exactly fits the politics model, because it emphasizes a step-by-step logical process in which the behavior of one set of people influences the next generation, which responds by changing its behavior, and thus unintentionally changes the situation for the next generation, and so on until the political system established by the philosopher-kings is wholly transformed. Plato's account is 'explanatory' in the true sense of scientific realism because it cuts open and exhibits the process, at the individual level, through which these events occur.

Allowances must be made by the modern reader for the first step in Plato's account, because it is said to occur when something goes wrong with the selection of the 'gold' children who should be identified in order to fill the highest places in the Republic. The explanation Plato gives for this error is mystical and can be ignored for present purposes. Believers in Murphy's Law, that 'if something can go wrong, it will,' can substitute that law as a modern equivalent for Plato's tortuous mathematical theory (546: b–d).

However it occurs, the apparently small problem in the selection of the elite rulers will begin to expand as it works its way through specific people. Because errors occur in their choosing, the 'best' people who are appointed to office are no longer worthy of their position, and when they reach the top of the political system, Plato says, they will neglect the needs of the people. Shortly discord will arise between the 'iron' and the 'bronze' types of citizen, who want private property, and the 'silver' and 'gold' people, who want to retain the traditional order based on excellence and justice.

As a compromise, property is distributed, and the political system becomes a timarchy (based on honor) where, according to Plato, authority is still respected and the soldier class maintains the old ideals of common community. But a deep change has occurred, because people now fear admitting intelligent people to office. Where once the intelligent were trained to be good, they are now considered dangerously clever. Timarchy values simple, hearty men who prefer the glories of war to more everyday activities.

Further Downhill

But human behavior creates not only a particular type of system, according to Plato's account, it creates unexpected side effects—and it creates critics. When philosophers no longer rule Plato's system, the state is badly run. As the young grow up, they see that their fathers, even if they are good men, are neither honored nor powerful, because they fail to succeed in the chaos of the law courts and politics. The mothers complain that their husbands' behavior deprives them of their rightful prestige, saying that they are too easygoing, 'not real men.'

The sons may admire their fathers, but in practical terms they see that the honors go to other types of behavior. The sons therefore resign themselves to a competitive life, becoming arrogant and ambitious. In such an oligarchy wealth is what counts. This is both its major characteristic and its major flaw. A property qualification is introduced for officeholding, and because, for Plato, wealth is not a good criterion for predicting talent at governing, the system further degenerates, splitting into rich and poor, who constantly plot against each other.

This preference for wealth arises, according to Plato, because the sons of the timarchs are frightened by the ease with which their fathers could be deposed when a political or military battle went against them. Money was considered to be a protection against the whims of fate, and Plato defines the oligarchic character as economical and hardworking—although the honesty of such men cannot be trusted.

The logic of further decline is based on this very desire for wealth, which soon breaks out of the bonds of restraint and takes over the rulers' whole character structure. They are unwilling to curtail the extravagance of the young because they get profits from lending money to those who run out of funds; they prefer extravagance also because it impoverishes citizens, and the poor are easier to govern. Eventually the rich become soft and weak, and the poor, who alone must struggle for an existence, become lean and hard.

'Democracy' (which the ancients thought of as a corrupt form of government) comes about in Plato's model because the young are led away from self-restraint into self-indulgence. They believe in complete individual freedom, that each person should arrange life as each thinks best. People no longer regard the laws and feel no compulsion either to rule or to obey. On the one hand, Plato says, this produces one of democracy's most attractive aspects, the diversity of character. But on the other hand, shame and self-control are mocked, and the community is characterized by insolence and license.

It is tempting to compare Plato's democracy with the voices heard in criticism of modern industrialized states at the end of the twentieth century: The demand for excessive liberty, according to Plato, ends the rule of law. Father stands in awe of son, no distinction is made between citizen and foreigner, teachers fear and pander to students, the young challenge their elders, the elders seek to appear young, and there is complete equality between the sexes. In this dreadful state of things, the people rally themselves behind some figurehead hero, who shortly becomes a tyrant.

Plato's account of political decline has various dramatic analogies in the present day, but we can for our purposes ignore the normative bent of the analysis. Notice rather that when Plato, the most classic of all political theorists, turned to the 'real' political world, he chose a politics model to describe it—a model in which the interactions of variously motivated individuals creates a context that in turn affects how other individuals act; and the interplay of basic human motives can be linked logically into dynamic chains of behavior that, when elucidated, provide explanations of events that might otherwise seem inexplicable. Political modeling thus did not begin recently, but long hence.

The Prince of Politics

Machiavelli's writings have, over the centuries, offended many political scientists and other people who have thought his analysis to be unduly harsh, and his conclusions absolutely dangerous. But other political scientists love these works for their ferocious clarity and their freedom from all sentimentality. It has become stylish to analyze Machiavelli's work to determine what he 'really' meant and whose side he was actually on, the prince's or the people's; but these issues are irrelevant here. The only important concern is with the inherent quality of the analysis, which turns up on page after page of both *The Prince* and *The Discourses*.

Take as an example one of Machiavelli's milder topics, the question raised while evaluating the necessary qualities of a prince, of 'whether it is better for a prince to be loved or feared.' Machiavelli quickly turns this value-laden question (what is 'better') to a scientific question, by changing a single word. I cannot tell you what is better, he says in effect, but I can tell you what is safer.

Once this little change has been effected, Machiavelli launches into his analysis, which within the space of a single paragraph provides an almost perfect example of what it means to follow the 'scientific realist' approach and strip away surfaces to get to the realities underneath. If reality is uncomfortable to the tender-minded, who prefer their illusions, it nonetheless has the authentic ring of truth.

As it would be unkind to paraphrase an explanation already so succinct, I give Machiavelli's own argument (Machiavelli 1940, 60–63). It is safer to be feared than loved, he says, because men in general

> are ungrateful, voluble, dissemblers, anxious to avoid danger, and covetous of gain; as long as you benefit them, they are entirely yours; they offer you their blood, their goods, their life, and their children . . . when the necessity is remote; but when it approaches, they revolt. And the prince who has relied entirely on their words, without making other preparations, is ruined; for the friendship which is gained by purchase and not through grandeur and nobility of spirit is bought but not secured, and at a pinch is not to be expended in your service.

Having stated these conclusions, Machiavelli descends deeper, to the fundamental principles on which they are based.

> And men have less scruple in offending one who makes himself loved than one who makes himself feared; for love is held by a chain of obligation which, men being selfish, is broken whenever it serves their purposes; but fear is maintained by a dread of punishment which never fails. (Chapter XVII)

To be feared, Machiavelli notes, is quite different from being hated, and the latter should be avoided. He concludes the chapter by restating his principle: "that men love at their own free will, but fear at the will of the prince, and that a wise prince must rely on what is in his power and not on what is in the power of others . . ." (Machiavelli 1940, 61–63).

The power of such an analysis lies in its simplicity. Wishful thinking is always tortuous, because the writer is trying to 'prove' something that is very likely impossible, such as that the world is full of cloud-capped castles where the rulers are wise and fair and the people strong, brave, and loyal. Machiavelli entirely lacks such a program, and he takes philosophical refuge in the only thing that can give him comfort, the picturing of reality as closely as he can perceive it. For those who take such a course, for those who try to catch up with political realities, Machiavelli's guidance is swift and sure—and simple, as science is often simple.

Lovers of Machiavelli may say I have tarnished his image, to put him in the same category as ordinary, modern political scientists. I would rather think of it as presenting a challenge to ordinary modern political scientists. In the context of his own time, place, and problems, Machiavelli's *The Prince* and *The Discourses of Titus Livius* demonstrate ideally the highest qualities of the politics model—to cut through the fuzziness of conventional thought to the jugular vein of politics, the hard interactions between governor and governed, the destructive and creative capacities of human nature, and the stubbornness and yet the fluidity of human institutions.

Now for the Present Century

Not to strain the reader's courtesy by spending too much time in the distant past, I skip over Rousseau's eminently concrete theory of 'the origins of inequality,' in which he describes how some men had the insolence to fence off for themselves what had hitherto been common property, and found others who were foolish enough to let them get away with it (Rousseau's Second Discourse). I also leave aside such competent nineteenth-century political theorists as Karl Marx, who showed in his discussion of the impact of England's corn laws on the length of the working day a subtle skill with the politics model.[4] This brings us to the early years of the twentieth century.

Here the politics model can be clearly discerned in two prebehavioral works: V. O. Key Jr.'s historical-descriptive study of parties and interest groups (1958), and Lasswell and Kaplan's massive effort at conceptual clarification in political theory (1950). On a superficial view, no two books could be less similar; to show, therefore, that each contains a wide range of the ideas that characterize the politics model is to give evidence of the prevalence and the power of the model, as well as insight into the variety of its applications to diverse areas of inquiry.[5]

V. O. Key Jr.'s preeminent position in the political science profession was a function of many things, including his flair for everyday politics (1949), his empiricism (1954), and his normative convictions (1966). For most political scientists, however, Key does not leap to mind as a political theorist. Yet one of his major works contains a clear statement of the politics model as defined here.

In *Politics, Parties, and Pressure Groups* (1958), Key focuses first on political *process* as covering "all sorts of efforts to guide, influence, or affect governmental action. The striving for power, for status, for privilege is never ending . . ." (Key 1958, 158). This is, of course, the defining core of the politics model. Parties, for Key, were not so much formal organizations as "amorphous institutions" where a "bewildering variety" of factions "struggle for supremacy" (Key 1958, 318). That there is any party unity at all depends not on the party apparatus but on "the social matrix within which the organization exists" and the political objectives created by scattered but similar social interests (Key 1958, 362). The "party" is defined by the "combination of social interests for which the party speaks" (Key 1958, 362). The dramatic difference between such an approach and the standard institutional analysis is obvious. In Key's analysis the institutions are not stable and solid but represent merely the surface of a bubbling pot, inside of which the real political events are located, out of sight.

The resultant political process is, according to Key, a collection of actors of varying degrees of organization, from "tightly knit clique[s] of political activists" to "pulverized" politics when candidates jump the party organization and develop their own loose coalitions of allies (Key 1958, 369). Democracy becomes, from this viewpoint, a mixture of oligarchies in constant pursuit of fluctuating political goals (Key 1958, 379). Internally the parties may be "dictatorial"; and intraparty competition tends to encourage one-party politics of "factions, cliques, and individuals with amorphous popular followings" (Key 1958, 380).

Key's analysis came to conclusions very different from the mainstream pluralist writers; his vision was harsher and closer to the facts. But the political science discipline was so enchanted by Key's wealth of historical detail that the theoretical quality of his work was lost to sight. In retrospect these elements are clear: (a) actors with (b) varying objectives and (c) resources, engaged in (d) dynamic processes of cooperation and competition, which (e) may not turn out exactly as the participants, or the observers, anticipated.[6]

Power and Politics

At the other end of the political science spectrum from Key's thick institutional description is Lasswell and Kaplan's *Power and Society* (1950). That it contains exactly the same theoretic framework as Key's analysis of grass-roots political parties provides convincing proof that the politics model has deep roots within the discipline. Readers may be familiar with the surface style of *Power and Society,* a formidable array of concepts, definitions, and propositions about political behavior, the complexity of which has perhaps discouraged the utilization of the work in political science research.

Lasswell and Kaplan's use of the same general framework used by Key is clear in the epigraphs and introductions to the several sections of the work.

> The subject matter of political science is constituted by the conduct of *persons* with various *perspectives* of action, and organized into *groups* of varying complexity. (Lasswell and Kaplan 1950, 1)

> Groups are formed by integrating diversified perspectives and operations. (Lasswell and Kaplan 1950, 29)

> By influence is meant the value position and potential of a person or group. (Lasswell and Kaplan 1950, 55)

> The power *process* is the pattern of all the political activities carried on in a given period. (Lasswell and Kaplan 1950, 175)

> Among the prominent features of the political processes are the rise and fall of political movements, and the occurrence and resolution of . . . crises. (Lasswell and Kaplan 1950, 240)

Lasswell stated the politics model in one of its most concise formulations as the title of his book *Who Gets What, When, How* (1958); but as Easton later noted, the text of Lasswell's book did not really answer the question posed by its title, being rather a study of elites. By placing Lasswell within the tradition of the politics model, one can better understand his place in the development of the political science discipline, a place that has often been obscured by the very originality and variety of his scholarly interests.[7]

The examples of Key and Lasswell, both showing use of the same basic elements leading to endlessly changing outcomes, serve as more evidence of the presence of the politics model in political science in the past, and of the ability of the model to undergird political analysis of widely differing types (Lave and March 1975; Merton 1957; Stinchcombe 1968).

In comparison with these two implicit and unrecognized general theorists, what distinguishes the 'recognized' theorists? David Easton provides an answer to this question in the first of his three influential works when, after describing the possibility of directing political science toward the study of actual political processes, he rejects this course of action. The process of the politics of government is, according to Easton, *not* what we are interested in.

> Although inescapable, our interest in politicking or the struggle for power is only derivative; it helps us to understand the kind of policy finally adopted for the society and the way in which such a policy has been put into effect. (Easton 1953, 128)

The belief that politics was "only derivative" led Easton into allocation theory and the abstractions of equilibrium analysis and "equilibrium polity"; the political scramble disappeared under the abstraction of the demand-and-support model (Easton 1953, 285, 293f; 1965).

Experience with the grand-systems viewpoint in subsequent decades did not speak favorably for the 'outputs' emphasis, however. Severe problems of application arose: Systems theory was either difficult to test (Sorzano 1975, 94), or, when operationalized, falsified (Chilcote 1981). But while the stylish debate went forward overhead, political analysis continued quietly underneath, using the intuitively more plausible politics model.

Concrete Theories of Ideas

A second step in the argument presented in this chapter is to show how concrete models can be created on the basis of existing descriptive studies. The case in point is a study of comparative political culture published during the behavioral period. The study (Pye and Verba 1965) was overshadowed by more stylish approaches that better fit the 'behavioral' canons of the time (Almond and Verba 1963). My analysis here shows that the substance of political culture can be put into scientific form, allowing its insights to be employed to direct further research across a much wider range of political behavior, in terms of the politics model.[8]

Political research frequently gains its primary force from the idea that it has uncovered new facts about the political world. This is a useful principle in that it encourages students of politics to go into real institutions, real organizations, real governments, real events, and to bring back interesting accounts of cases and people that have been hitherto overlooked. But the principle of 'facts are important' often slights the contribution to political understanding that is made by the application of new ideas to old facts.

The principle of 'models are important' needs to be added to research principles in political science to complement the collection of facts with the increase of understanding. Much apparently traditional research contains all the elements necessary to the construction of empirical political theories or models. In the present instance I would like to show that apparently 'traditional' anthropological approaches to political culture can be easily converted into concrete models of ideas.

The concept of political culture has been important in political science as perhaps the only vehicle for the analytic study of political ideas, the importance of which everyone admits, but the description of which has proved difficult. Political culture studies were a major focus of the early behavioral period in political science, but they were hampered by a set of normative concerns—that 'cultured' citizens would create or improve upon democracy as a form of government, or that cultures could be manipulated in order to increase the rate of national development.

Adopting the strategy of applying the politics model to already existing materials, I try to show here how the politics model can be empirically and logically grounded in the individual idea systems of different political cultures. In each case I take the materials provided in the book *Political Culture and Political Development* (Pye and Verba 1965) and reorder them into explicit models. These serve both to explain behavior in the separate cultures and to provide a ground for operational models of decision under different types of rules (Lane 1992).

Indian Political Culture

A first example of the concrete approach to idea systems is found in the wide-ranging and acute analysis of Indian political culture in which Weiner (1965) begins by observing that there are two major political cultures in India, the mass and the elite, but that, contrary to expectations, this is not the same as the distinction between traditional and modern. Rather there is much that is quintessentially 'modern' and fiercely democratic about local politics. Despite the fact that India is a hierarchical society in which "authority is esteemed" (Weiner 1965,

208), the political behavior of village India does not demonstrate the authoritarian attitudes such a term might lead one to expect. Rather local Indian politics demonstrates a scramble for office, higher turnout at the polls in local elections than in national contests, and a vigorous adherence to the claims of parochial self-interest.

Weiner's syllogism allows us to unfold the apparent inconsistency: India is hierarchical and authority is esteemed, but some unstated factor means that individuals seek the available power positions themselves, rather than remaining in their lower positions (Weiner 1965, 208–9). In other words, the hierarchy is accepted but not the incumbents of the hierarchical positions, apparently because of an individualistic tradition that encourages active political persons in a kind of constant ambition. Weiner gives no direct support for suggesting that village India makes the individual more important than the group; but he does observe the loss of the 'saintly' tradition of "harmony, unanimity, and sacrifice." We are therefore allowed to conclude, tentatively, that individualism is at least one of the values that distinguishes the culture of village India from that of a more typical authoritarian system.

Amhara Political Culture

To turn, in the search for models of idea systems that can be made useful as a basis for the politics framework, to Levine's analysis of Ethiopia (1965, 245–81) is to be sharply reminded of the hazards of cross-cultural comparison. For in the elite Amhara culture, one finds again a strong hierarchical norm, but one that is combined with other beliefs to produce an absolute, emperor-oriented autocracy. This is somewhat surprising because the Amhara believe that the individual is more important than the group, and this might be expected to produce a pattern somewhat resembling India. But this is not the case.

Authority is particularly pervasive in Amhara culture, according to Levine's account; in its absence there are acute psychological symptoms of incompleteness and malaise (Levine 1965, 250). Deference to superiors is complete, widespread, and inculcated early. The hierarchy depends upon a conception of human nature that is "radically un-egalitarian," ranked sharply according to age, sex, ethnic identification, religion, wealth, and social position (Levine 1965, 257, 251).

Where there is conflict between the group and the individual, how-ever, the individual is given preference. Amharic has no word to denote 'community,' and even where social problems arise individuals do not attempt to unite as a group in order to solve them (Levine 1965, 262, 261). That the Amharic cultural viewpoint is unlike the Indian is a function of the Amhara definition of human nature: "man's inherent aggressiveness and his untrustworthiness"; without strict training he will be "rude . . . tending to trample on others" (Levine 1965, 258).

The logic is, in summary, (1) the individual is more important than the community (as in Indian practice), (2) the individual is considered dangerous (which is unlike the Indian case), and (3) ergo, strong rule is needed to maintain any semblance of order. This is a particularly good example of the way in which idea systems, typically thought of as impossible to analyze, can be opened up through the application of the politics approach, laying bare the internal logic that explains their surface meaning.

Japanese Political Culture

Ward's (1965, 27–82) analysis of Japanese political culture provides another example of the range of options in the idea systems that ground applications of the politics model. It also demonstrates how modern cultures may be deeply rooted in traditional attitudes. The basic social definitions in traditional Japanese culture were based on economic stratification (the nobility, the samurai warrior class, the merchants, the artisans, and the peasants) upon which were built normative roles. The upper classes had rights, the lower ones had duties: the nobility engaged in 'high decision making,' the warriors in administration and defense. The other three classes shared a single political role, that of loyalty, support, and obedience, as well as an acceptance that they were to stay out of political decisions.[9]

Modernization brought to Japan a continuation of the traditional Tokugawa political culture, with modifications designed to improve its economic and social functioning. Ward quotes from a revealing "Rescript on Education" of 1890 (said to have "set the tone" until 1945) that exhorts the people to pursue filial and social pieties, arts and learning, and moral perfection. In respect to any specifically political duties, the Rescript prescribed loyalty to the constitution, the promotion of common interests, and physical self-sacrifice in national emergencies. It made no mention of participation in political affairs.

For the Japan of the 1960s, the time at which he wrote, Ward defined a less prescriptive political culture, presumably superimposed upon the older elements. Elements of this political culture included a kind of narcissistic nationalism, a demand for group harmony and consensual decision making, and expectations that the government would 'produce' social goods, individuals who were 'apathetic' and worked only through groups, and a pervasive, virulent factionalism.[10]

Formalization of these beliefs requires again that deeper levels be tapped, since the surface values are in contradiction—for instance, the apparent incompatibility of the ideals of group harmony and intense factionalism. The formalized principles include:

1. The group is more important than the individual. Therefore the individual alone is weak ('apathetic').
2. Political society is made up of groups. Therefore the individual gains strength by joining the group.
3. Group members' duties are loyalty. Because (by 1 and 2) without loyalty the group will dissolve and the individual will be left powerless.
4. Enemies must be destroyed. Because (as in 3) loss of group is loss of individual power.
5. The leader is absolute so long as he furthers the interests of the group.

English Political Culture

A final example of secondary analysis of political culture shows that a radical analysis of political ideas can, in effect, become a 'politics model' of a whole nation. Rose's analysis of English political culture, which is refreshing in its dismissal of many old pieties, results from his decision to reinterpret English political culture in terms of pure elitism.

Though England is generally considered the mother of democracies, Rose's analysis shows that most of the values commonly cited as components of English political culture are values only for the elite groups. In the first place, there is a traditional English belief that government is beneficent—at least, as Rose notes, "for some groups" (Rose 1965, 93). The belief in liberty also discloses an elitist meaning: Because the belief was held along with a horror of the 'masses' and the practice of a very narrow franchise, it meant, in effect, liberty only for the ruling classes. The norm of limited government was also elitist, according to Rose, the result of the fears of those members of the upper classes who were outside of court circles and sought to protect themselves from court insiders (Rose 1965, 97).

Other 'English' values that are actually 'English upper-class' values include: 'privacy' in government, which means the elites make government policy without citizen scrutiny; 'trust in fellow citizens,' meaning adherence to the elite values of feudal societies; the 'gentleman' syndrome of officeholding by nonspecialists; and 'consultation among decision makers,' which takes place wholly at the elite level (Rose 1965 96, 97). The major 'right' of the masses is deference.

Reconciling 'liberty' and 'deference' frequently perplexes observers, Rose suggests; but the harmony is plain when the whole English system is understood. The logic of the political system is straightforward: Deference increases liberty, according to Rose, because it makes leaders feel more secure in office. Since the English upper classes are defined as 'more lazy than autocratic' (that is, they are not inherently tyrannical), the only thing that might make them behave so would be their fear of the masses. When the masses are deferential, fear is unnecessary, and government is easy. This is convincing and quite in accord with the 'civic culture' conclusions; but certainly the logic is harsher and more 'realist' than any found in civic culture studies.[11]

The British culture, reduced to some of its most basic principles, might be as follows:

1. Elite individuals are more important than nonelite individuals.
2. Elite individuals have rights, among them the maximization of personal perquisites and profits. Nonelites have duties, primary among which is obedience to elites.
3. Elite individuals can increase their gains by cooperation among themselves.
4. Elites must especially guard against letting any other groups get out of control, specifically:
   a. Strict controls must be placed on the monarch.
   b. In respect to the masses, the elite must
      i. encourage their deference by seeming to deserve it;
      ii. act so as to be useful to them (by administering law, etc.); and
      iii. avoid driving them to desperation.
   c. Talented upstarts must be assimilated.

In sum, the English system looks less like a classic democracy and more like a domestic 'balance of power' system: firm, flexible, well tempered.

The concrete analysis of political ideas shows the same quality as do other applications of the politics model: Deeper principles are uncovered, and these change our understanding of the surface events.

Case Research Is Not the Politics Model

The final step in the series of arguments made in this chapter is an attempt to quell an easy misinterpretation: that simple historical description, or even strong conceptual analysis, is sufficient for a work of research to be designated as exemplifying the politics model. Such an interpretation is false because, as shown more fully in Chapter 6, the tenets of scientific realism are extremely rigorous—more rigorous than those of positivism and certainly more rigorous than those of the traditional political science past. I present two examples, both much admired, to show that empirical and analytical description both leave out the essence of concrete theory: the emphasis on the logical connectedness of significant events, and the construction of an explanatory web.

The approach taken in concrete theories of politics and the more extensive analyses based on the full politics model can lead, if care is not taken, to a serious error—the idea that political science can go back to historical description and to idiographic case studies. This is exactly the wrong conclusion to draw. For one thing, a science can never really go 'backward'; when practices that once seemed legitimate are superseded, they never again can acquire the legitimacy necessary to attract research interest. Now that political science has spent some forty years agonizing over its data and its statistical models, the old approach to political history has become meaningless.

The important point about the politics model is that it does not represent an 'easier' way of life than positivism, but a more rigorous one; not an 'escape' from the rigors of empirical science, but a fuller, better description of how science actually operates. Only to the superficial reader do the examples of concrete theory discussed earlier resemble prebehavioral approaches. Scientific realism—which defines, explains, and justifies the politics model—is more, rather than less, scientific than both the older prepositivist approach and the positivist approach itself (see Chapter 6).

As a way of emphasizing the difference between descriptive or analytic history and the politics model, I first study two admirable examples of political inquiry. The first case is an absorbing study of U.S. tax reform during the Reagan administration (Birnbaum and Murray 1987) that delves so deeply into the details of the political process on Capitol Hill and in the White House that the reader feels almost a participant—one expects at any moment to be told the color of the socks an important congressman was wearing.

But the theoretic integrity of the politics model requires that this sort of high journalistic description, however full of facts and insights, be distinguished from it. After outlining the reported events, therefore, I suggest what the authors have 'left out' in terms of the requirements of the politics model.

A second example of the way in which even close analysis of political events may be different from the politics model is the 'development state' approach summarized in Onis (1991). Here the conceptualization is extensive and lays out a strong and clear framework of the conditions and behaviors involved in rapid economic development. Despite this, however, the description is not sufficiently dynamic to qualify as an example of the politics model, and it leaves important issues untreated. In this case, as with the first example, my point is not to complain about the quality of the research—the quality of both is of the first order. But it is important to the present argument that the politics model be understood in its distinctness.

The Politics Model Is Not Just Politics

The approach of the widely known study of the 1986 Reagan Tax Reform Act (Birnbaum and Murray 1987) may seem similar to works identified above with the politics model, for it is a detailed study of the intricate steps by which tax reform emerged, developed, and finally succeeded. Indeed, a major player in the reform process is quoted by the publisher on the opening page as affirming that the book is a comprehensive guide "to how the sausage is made up here." Since I have inadvertently used the sausage metaphor as a characteristic of the politics model, a book so described must present a prima facie claim to be included.

The Birnbaum and Murray case study is marked, however, by a remarkably high degree of discontinuity. Almost none of the officials who proposed, advocated, or voted for the Tax Reform Act of 1986 had any interest in tax reform; nor did the polls show any public interest. Instead an idea put forth by a single congressman is swept by almost random forces to its successful conclusion. As the tale is told by Birnbaum and Murray, the proposal was first taken up by President Reagan because of a mistake: It was believed, incorrectly, in the White House that Mondale might try to use it in the presidential campaign. This brief sponsorship died with the end of the campaign, but was revived when Reagan's secretary of the Treasury took it up; motivated by a desire to achieve more prestige in the White House, he supported a radical bill primarily because he enjoyed 'shaking up the establishment' (1987, 44). No one was keen on the Treasury plan, but then for entirely unrelated reasons, the Treasury secretary and the chief of staff switched jobs; this meant that the old Treasury secretary now had the ear of the president, and meant also that the new secretary was a renowned political operator who could pull the strings to get the bill moving. The bill then went to the House, where the Ways and Means Committee chairman took it up reluctantly (not being a known proponent of reform) and did so largely because the Democratic Party needed, he thought, a big issue to wipe out the stigma of the recent loss in the presidential election. The White House had by now gotten tired of the bill, but when Ways and Means Republicans defied the chairman because they felt harassed by their minority status in the House, Reagan strategists supported the bill as a matter of reasserting leadership.

Sent to the Senate Finance Committee, the bill encountered a committee and a chairman with no enthusiasm for tax reform. But the chairman was reluctant to oppose a president from his own party, and he was concerned not to do anything that might hurt his own reelection chances (1987, 189–90). The first Senate bill was so riddled with new loopholes that it embarrassed the committee. But fearing to let 'reform' die on his watch, the committee chairman invented a second bill so radical (reducing all rates below 30 percent) that it caught opponents off guard and acquired a momentum of its own (206–7). The president was unaware of most of the provisions of the bill and had to be coaxed to support it.

The Question of Conclusions

The primary lesson the authors derive from this intriguing history is that "the special interests sometimes lose" (1987, 287). But the narrative gives no clue as to why this conclusion came about, nor to how it might be repeated; indeed, the suggestion is rather that Congress will probably gut the reform at its next session (1987, 290). All this is certainly politics. Is it the politics model?

The most striking feature of the Birnbaum and Murray history of the Tax Reform Act of 1986 is its unpredictability. Nothing seems to happen twice, no forces are constant, no individual (except perhaps for the originator of the idea of the tax reform) behaves with any regularity. Sometimes the congressmen were motivated by their desire for reelection and for campaign funds, but on other occasions everyone might equally have been motivated by loyalty to a hard-pressed chairman, by duty in taking over the work of an office, by sympathy for colleagues, by the desire for reputation, by the 'charm' of a particular legislator, or by petty greed.

Even where 'rational' action was feasible (it was said that if the bill's opponents had just gotten together they could have defeated it), it did not occur. Almost no one was motivated by any interest in tax reform itself.[12] In addition, the history contains numerous 'random' elements that changed the course of the bill. When, for instance, an expert from the tax office said, "You can't do that, it will be complex to administer," a provision was dropped, or sometimes the expert's arm was twisted to reverse his original opinion. Thus while the Birnbaum and Murray history is microanalytic and emphasizes interactive process, as does the politics model, it lacks connectedness and the resulting depth of explanation that is so important in the politics model.

But, the reader may protest, the 1986 Tax Reform Act was an atypical case, of which no one could build a theory; therefore you have not proved that the politics model is more than just politics. Perhaps your 'politics model' theorists simply chose more orderly situations to describe. This is a fair criticism and must be answered.

How might this tax-reform case have been treated by persons who employ the politics model? We might take for an example the work of Huntington (1968), which can be utilized here despite the distance between Third World nation building and U.S. tax policy, because of the politics model's strong theoretical core. Huntington might begin a theoretical treatment along lines of his "the rich bribe . . . the students riot," or, in other words, we must pay attention to how different actors use the 'resources' that their talents and positions give them. In the tax case, the 'experts' played a major role (which the authors do not systematically evaluate) in presenting different policy elements to the politicians. Or, for a second instance, one might select the example of Migdal (1988), who would have focused on the 'strategies of survival' utilized by the various players—the relationship between, say, congressmen and favored aides to devise policies in order to win favor from their employers or observers. Polsby (1983) might have focused on the dynamics inherent in the policy itself, how it acquired supporters by its relationship to existing ideologies. So it is not the facts which are atheoretical, but the treatment. Practitioners of the politics model would have drawn connections, highlighted certain events, inquired into underlying structures.

Nor Is Logic Enough

Our first 'negative case' therefore shows that pure politics is not the same as the politics model. Yet the test may seem too easy, focusing on a work that won a prize from the American Political Science Association but was not written by professional political scientists. The second test case is therefore of a different sort, an article appearing in a major political science journal, which has attracted attention both for its subject matter, the so-called developmental state, and for its method of analysis, which is conceptual and alert to the configuration of factors influencing actors' behavior. The author also proposes his 'institutional' perspective as a new one, transcending both early structuralist development theory and neoclassical liberalism (Onis 1991, 110).

The strategic industrial policy that forms a main component of the developmental state model in rapidly developing East Asian nations is characterized by "very high levels of investment, more investment in certain key industries than would have occurred in the absence of government intervention, and exposure of many industries to international competition in foreign markets" (Onis 1991, 111–12). These characteristics are traced back to a more fundamental set of policies by which elites guided or governed resource allocation in a manner different from what the free market would produce, and then further back to two central features, "the unusual degrees of bureaucratic autonomy and public-private cooperation."

Going Beyond Description

The puzzling feature of this pattern is, as Onis notes, "how bureaucratic autonomy was acquired in the first place and why it was subsequently directed to developmental goals as opposed to the self-maximizing or predatory forms of behavior so common in other contexts" (1991, 114). The answer lies in meritocratic procedures of recruitment and training, extreme limits on the size of the bureaucracy, creation of pilot agencies, rule by the bureaucracy (while politicians only reign), and student protests to check malfeasance. This constitutes the "logic of the developmental state" (1991, 115).

But it does not explain why these features have been created. Two factors are suggested to provide a deeper level of explanation. The first is geopolitical: external security threats and resource scarcity. The second is socioeconomic: that each of the East Asian states "experienced a major redistribution of income and wealth from the outset, with the corollary that the industrialization drive in the postwar period has been initiated from a relatively egalitarian base" (Onis 1991, 116–17). Here the description of the developmental state 'model' stops, leaving a fund of interesting possibilities but no connections.

First, one wants to know the purposes and circumstances of the elite actors: What was their initial position in society? What norms aided or constrained them? Did their intentions succeed in the way that was originally intended? Second, the 'developmental logic' of the developmental state needs clarification: How did the purposes of the various actors mesh? What specific configuration of circumstances surrounded the substages in the process?

The 'politics model' would have placed emphasis on these dynamic, political, empirical connections; Onis's developmental model instead presents the reader with an apparently successful outcome (the developmental state) with little detailed information on how the outcome was achieved or on the actual operation of the political forces at work. This is not to be understood as criticism of the author. My concern is rather to show, by giving examples of excellent research in politics and state behavior that do not achieve the depth explanations produced by the politics model, that the politics model *is a model,* not merely an emphasis on political behavior.

Eggs, Stones, and Theories

Mao Zedong once enunciated the striking principle, which the rest of us might not have noticed unless it were pointed out, that the difference between an egg and a stone is that only one of them can be turned into a chicken.[13] In a loose sense that has been the principle also of the present chapter, which has sought to show that the politics model presented here is not an artificial invention but a real method that has life and substance and has existed over a considerable period of time, from Plato and Machiavelli, to the lost generation of political scientists that prepared the way for the behavioral revolution and modern political science, to the present.

The behavioral generation of political scientists took a different approach to method and theory. Discontented with 'the past,' many writers felt it appropriate to reject that past completely and to 'invent' what seemed to be entirely new approaches to the study of politics. These 'frameworks,' 'approaches,' and 'theories' were often ingenious and often plausible, but they were fundamentally stones rather than eggs: They prescribed ideas based on superficial political analogies, and then urged other political scientists to take these ideas out and try their efficacy on actual political problems. To a surprising degree many in the audience did declare themselves adherents to the ideas, did take the new concepts out into the various sections of the political world and seek to apply them. An important example of this phenomenon is examined in the next chapter.

Frequently, however, these 'invented' solutions failed, sooner or later. Some were too abstract to be intelligibly applied to anything as mundane as politics. Others were too narrow to encompass the rich peculiarities of politics. Others provided only new labels to pin on old facts but otherwise offered little in the way of theory or explanation. Political scientists, by seeking to short-cut the natural course of scientific development and to progress too far, too fast, lost their natural sense of the subject matter of politics. Rather than starting with basics, figuring out what was the natural unit of analysis, and delving directly into politics, many in the political science community set up ambitious and idealized goals and sought to become physicists overnight. Others, in defiance, refused to consider science as feasible at all and stuck by their traditional norms. The standoff exists even today, in some places.

But other political scientists, the subject of the present work, found it appropriate and convenient, when faced with the real political world, to adopt a 'natural' method of studying men and women in their strategically patterned interactions. Often these theorists thought the method they used was exclusively their own; equally often they did not conceive of their approach as a method at all; certainly no one claimed it as a new analytic path for political science. The whole situation might provide an interesting chapter in the history of the sciences because it suggests that a scientific consensus may emerge without anyone's paying any attention to it, and a model may develop not by prescription but by natural growth. .

By showing that the politics model (1) has ancient and honorable roots in traditional political theory, (2) can encourage a secondary analysis of qualitative studies that turns them into scientific form and (3) pushes political scientists further to use their rich descriptions as the basis for a 'politics model,' the present chapter has tried to argue that the new approach is an egg and not a stone, a thing not merely round and pretty, but instinct with life.

Notes

Some of the materials included in this chapter appeared originally in *Comparative Political Studies* 25, no. 3 (October 1992): 362–87, copyright © 1992 by Comparative Political Studies. Reprinted by permission of Sage Publications.

1. The one other member of the panel voted for Woodrow Wilson as the father of political science. Some observers felt that this result was interesting, but the majority agreed it was not statistically significant.

2. Gunnell also suggests that these 'great' disciplinary ancestors are not the proper fathers of the discipline, but that a 'real' history of political science would involve the names of obscure (and sometimes imperialist or racist) writers such as Burgess, Goodnow, and Willoughby (Gunnell 1991, 14–15).

3. Bluhm (1971) attempted a synthesis between the ancient and the modern, using such pairs as Thucydides and Weber, Plato and Strauss, Aristotle and Lipset, Machiavelli and Neustadt, Hobbes and Downs and Riker; but this approach did not take hold during the behavioral period.

4. Marx's *Capital* (vol. 1, 1867) is too little read as an analytic exercise. Chapter 10 of that work, "The Working Day," shows vividly how the shortening of the working day for children and women was the result not of some sentimental desire to improve the lot of the working poor, but of the fact that when the Chartists brought the issue to the House of Commons in 1846–1847, they found the Tories their allies because the repeal of the Corn Laws, which supported the prices landowners got for their produce, had left the Tories "panting for revenge" against the manufacturers (Marx 1967, 283). This is exactly the kind of 'politics' involved in the politics model: Actors may vote for a program not because of their

beliefs about its inherent merits but because they wish to damage an enemy from a previous battle.

5. This similarity may be attributed to a common background at the University of Chicago, but this background is itself ambiguous. The 'Chicago School' was perceived by outsiders to have a strong methodological and substantive unity, yet a recent oral history compilation (Baer, Jewell, and Sigelman 1991) undercuts this supposed homogeneity and the intellectual leadership of Merriam by showing how differently the Chicago School appeared depending on when one arrived and with whom one associated. Histories and reminiscences of the period agree that Merriam's role in the development of political science, massively important though it was, centered on his entrepreneurial skills rather than his intellectual leadership. Merriam's lasting importance for political science was to be in his students and in the institutional framework he provided to encourage the research of these students and other members of the discipline. Even among his students, however, Merriam's influence was an ambiguous one. One historian points out that as Merriam moved in his eclecticism from one method to another, each student "tended to adopt one of the methods with which Merriam toyed," so that each went in a different direction (Karl 1974, 114). Gabriel Almond, a student at the University of Chicago from 1932 to 1938, recalled that Merriam's concern was a unique combination of science, civic activity, and morality that did not culminate in any single theoretical work. Almond recounted that "it was his [Merriam's] ambition that somehow he'd pull all this together when he retired, but when he thought, 'Now I'm going to sit down and do the *Gemeine Staatslehre*,' it just didn't come. In that sense, he felt that his life wasn't fulfilled" (Almond in Baer, Jewell, and Sigelman 1991, 124). Tsou (1955), who is said to have made the greatest attempt to find a unified theoretical structure in Merriam (Karl 1974, x), emphasizes the shallowness of Merriam's philosophical foundations, his concern with "the moral basis of power," and his ultimate shift away from the scientific viewpoint (Tsou 1955, 16, 25).

6. This description of Key's theory may remind some readers of Arthur F. Bentley's *Process of Government,* but it should be remembered that Bentley's work was journalistic and antiformalistic, whereas Key's purpose was scientific. Bentley's work is ably discussed by Seidelman (1985, 67–80).

7. In discussing Lasswell's work, Easton said (1953, 120): "The title of this book represents his most general conception of the subject of political science. . . . In terms of the actual problems that were explored in this work, however, the title appears somewhat overambitious. It does not really mirror the contents lying between its covers. It bears the promise that the author will discuss how social values are distributed in society. . . . In fact, however, it is devoted to exploring the sources of power held by a political elite."

8. The Pye and Verba volume partially overlapped the earlier Almond and Verba volume in discussing the political cultures of nations treated there, such as Germany, Italy, and Mexico. In these cases the treatment was positivist, emphasizing survey research. My present discussion focuses not on these cases but the other, 'softer' chapters.

9. The Japanese experience makes particularly plain the way in which what is often called 'the' political culture is merely the culture of the ruling classes. As Ward shows, the masses agreed upon the raw fact of the class stratification, but

instead of seeing it as a rational hierarchy, they saw it as exploitative; and they defined their role not as loyalty but as escape—to avoid government whenever possible.

10. The analysis emphasizes the importance of not imposing the observer's cultural preconceptions on the culture he or she is observing. Rather than seeing themselves as individually apathetic, the Japanese might reasonably see themselves as energetic and practical: The importance of groups, plus the unimportance attributed to individuals, may lead to the reasonable conclusion that 'if I want to get something, I had better join a group in order to succeed in getting it.'

11. The only other specifically nonelite value, in addition to deference, is 'welfare.' Rose's references make clear it is not only a relatively recent value, but one which arouses much controversy (Rose 1965, 98).

12. The bill had an inherent interest of its own, but the relationship between its particular provisions and the politics of its adoptions is not investigated in any theoretic way by the authors. The proposal that became the Tax Reform Act of 1986 was based on the idea of 'nonpartisan' reform that would attract Democratic Party support by eliminating loopholes for the rich, and would attract Republicans by decreasing the tax rates for top income categories. In addition it was to benefit taxpayers by making the system fairer and more understandable (1987, 23). The idea intersected, in ways not analyzed by the authors, with the nation's increasing deficits after the 1981 tax cuts, the inability to close tax loopholes because of interest groups' strength, and the rise of 'supply side' economics.

13. For Mao's discussion see *Selected Readings from the Works of Mao Tsetung* (1971).

References

Almond, Gabriel A., and Sidney Verba. 1963. *The Civic Culture*. Princeton, NJ: Princeton University Press.

Baer, Michael A., Malcolm E. Jewell, and Lee Sigelman, eds. 1991. *Political Science in America: Oral Histories of a Discipline*. Lexington: University Press of Kentucky.

Bentley, Arthur F. [1908] 1987. *The Process of Government*. Cambridge, MA: Harvard University Press.

Birnbaum, Jeffrey H., and Alan S. Murray. 1987. *Showdown at Guggi Gulch: Lawmakers, Lobbyists and the Unlikely Triumph of Tax Reform*. New York: Vintage.

Bluhm, William T. 1971. *Theories of the Political System: Classics of Political Thought and Modern Political Analysis*. Englewood Cliffs, NJ: Prentice Hall.

Chilcote, Ronald H. 1981. *Theories of Comparative Politics: The Search for a Paradigm*. Boulder, CO: Westview Press.

Easton, David. [1953] 1964. *The Political System: An Inquiry into the State of Political Science*. Chicago: University of Chicago Press.

———. 1965. *A Systems Analysis of Political Life*. New York: John Wiley and Sons.

Gunnell, John G. 1986. *Between Philosophy and Politics: The Alienation of Political Theory*. Amherst: University of Massachusetts Press.

———. 1991. "The Historiography of American Political Science." In *The Development of Political Science: A Comparative Survey,* ed. David Easton, John G. Gunnell, and Luigi Graziano, pp. 13–33. London: Routledge.

Huntington, Samuel P. 1968. *Political Order in Changing Societies.* New Haven, CT: Yale University Press.

Karl, Barry D. 1974. *Charles E. Merriam and the Study of Politics.* Chicago: University of Chicago Press.

Key, Vladimir Orlando, Jr. 1949. *Southern Politics in State and Nation.* New York: Knopf.

———. 1958. *Politics, Parties, and Pressure Groups.* 4th ed. New York: Crowell.

———. 1954. *A Primer of Statistics for Political Scientists.* New York: Crowell.

———. 1966. *The Responsible Electorate: Rationality in Presidential Voting 1936–1960.* Cambridge, MA: Harvard University Press.

Lane, Ruth. 1962. "Political Culture: Residual Category or General Theory?" *Comparative Political Studies* 25, no. 3 (October): 362–87.

Lasswell, Harold D. 1958. *Politics: Who Gets What, When, How.* Cleveland: World Publishing Company.

Lasswell, Harold D., and Abraham Kaplan. 1950. *Power and Society: A Framework for Political Inquiry.* New Haven, CT: Yale University Press.

Lave, Charles A., and James G. March. 1975. *An Introduction to Models in the Social Sciences.* New York: Harper and Row.

Levine, Donald N. 1965. "Ethiopia: Identity, Authority, and Realism." In Pye and Verba 1965, pp. 245–81.

Machiavelli, Niccolo. 1940. *The Prince and the Discourses.* New York: The Modern Library.

Mao Tse-tung. 1971. *Selected Readings from the Works of Mao Tsetung.* Peking: Foreign Languages Press.

Marx, Karl. [1867] 1967. *Capital Volume I: A Critical Analysis of Capitalist Production (1867),* Edited by F. Engels. New York: International Publishers.

Merton, Robert K. [1949] 1957. *Social Theory and Social Structure.* New York: The Free Press.

Migdal, Joel S. 1988. *Strong Societies and Weak States: State–Society Relations and State Capabilities in the Third World.* Princeton, NJ: Princeton University Press.

Onis, Ziya. 1991. "The Logic of the Developmental State." *Comparative Politics* 24, no. 1 (October) 109–26.

Plato. 1987. *The Republic.* Translated by Desmond Lee. New York: Penguin.

Pye, Lucien W., and Sidney Verba, eds. 1965. *Political Culture and Political Development.* Princeton, NJ: Princeton University Press.

Rose, Richard. 1965. "England: The Traditionally Modern Political Culture." In Pye and Verba 1965, pp. 83–129.

Rousseau, Jean-Jacques. 1964. *The First and Second Discourses.* New York: St. Martin's Press.

Seidelman, Raymond, with Edward J. Harpham. 1985. *Disenchanted Realists: Political Science and the American Crisis 1884–1984.* Albany, NY: SUNY Press.

Sorzano, J. S. 1975. "David Easton and the Invisible Hand." *American Political Science Review* 69, no. 1 (March): 91–106.

Stinchcombe, Arthur L. 1968. *Constructing Social Theories*. New York: Harcourt, Brace, World.

Tsou, Tang. 1955–56. "Fact and Value in Charles E. Merriam." *Southwestern Social Science Quarterly* 36:9–26.

Ward, Robert E. 1965. "Japan: The Continuity of Modernization." In Pye and Verba 1965, pp. 27–82.

Weiner, Myron. 1965. "India: Two Political Cultures." In Pye and Verba 1965, pp. 199–244.

5 GRAND THEORY AND A CONCRETE MODEL

Political scientists have an ambivalent attitude toward theory, combining the most sanguine of hopes that a good theory will solve all their problems with a grouchy anticipation of betrayal, a fear that the theory will fail to live up to its responsibilities and waste the efforts of its followers. In this nervous relationship, political scientists are apt to throw themselves wholesale into some new theoretical vision, and then roughly discard it when the first flaws or shortcomings appear. The attitude is romantic rather than scientific.

Theories should properly be evaluated not as solutions but as beginnings. A good idea need not necessarily be a perfect idea; it is rather a cognitive mechanism that leads one to think in interesting new ways about old problems. If a theory fails, the answer is not to cast it to the winds but to improve upon it. Often this can be done in small, constructive ways; other times it may require a complete inversion of analytic style in order to retain the inner meaning of the theory while making it more applicable in daily research.

The present chapter proceeds in its inquiry into the politics model by reconsidering an old, highly touted theory with the inconveniently long name of structural-functionalism, borrowed by political scientists from sociology, and a mainstay of the comparative politics field for a considerable period of time. The basic idea of structural-functionalism was that whole political or social systems could be understood as functional unities, in which certain needs were fulfilled by certain structures; such as, for instance, the heart fulfills its systemic function by causing blood to circulate through the body. Structural-functionalism claimed attention from political scientists on the grounds that a comparative analysis of political institutions would forever be impossible because every nation had institutions that were so utterly different from any other nation's that the mind boggled. A functional approach seemed to transcend this problem by focusing on functions common to all systems.

On the surface, the history of functionalism in political science seems short and decisive: It was launched in 1960 (Almond and Coleman), formed the basis of a nine-volume series of books in political development put out by a distinguished university publisher,[1] was vigorously criticized in a 1975 article (Holt and Turner), and has been presumed dead ever since. In this apparently rapid rise and fall of a highly abstract theory is hidden a circumstance that is odd and interesting in terms of the politics model. The circumstance, to make a long tale short, is that while proclaiming adherence to structural-functionalism, the group of authors who made the culminating statement of the theory (Binder et al. 1971) in fact spent at least half their time not using the structural-functional model at all. When push came to shove, when the authors wanted to say something coherent about the politics of development, they turned to a model that cannot be better described than to call it the politics model. This might seem of interest only for a desultory inquiry in the history of ideas, but that would be a mistake. Functionalism was an excellent idea; the question only was how best to implement it.

The lesson of the present chapter illustrates a constructive approach to research theory in political science, a turning away from the romantic 'all or nothing' approach in favor of a practical attitude. Instead of asking whether a given theory solves all problems, a scientific approach asks merely whether there are any good ideas in the theory, and, if so, how they can be extracted and put to use. Since political science contains a good many intelligent people, the theories they employ are almost always useful in some way or another; it is largely a matter of how much diligence one expends. The challenge is increased by the fact that gold is sometimes hidden in unexpected places.

A second concern of course infuses this inquiry, which is the evaluation of the politics model within political science. As the subsequent discussion suggests, in the case of structural-functionalism the politics model had to fight against the highest and most stylish brand of social science paradigm. And it would not be any real exaggeration to say that the politics model won. Analysts who tried to adhere to the abstract canons of functionalism found themselves, when it came time to do hard analysis, using the methods characteristic of the politics model, decomposing whole systems into their parts, showing the logic of interaction between actors with different goals and resources, and drawing sometimes unexpected conclusions with reference to political development. It seems a tribute to political scientists' common sense that, in the teeth of paradigmatic encouragement to do 'higher' theory, they still 'naturally' preferred the politics model.

The value of this reanalysis of structural-functionalism from a concrete viewpoint lies not only in the way it increases the observer's understanding of both functionalism and the politics model, but in the possibility that functionalism can be reinterpreted from the bottom up, instead of the top down, to form a sort of empirical theory that emphasizes system needs and their fulfillment but does so at an operational level where measurement and testing are possible.

Functional Backgrounds

The history of structural-functionalism within political science was mediated in important ways by specific persons and institutions. Functionalism, to begin with, was not a single movement even in sociology; it encompassed the quite different perspectives of Talcott Parsons and Robert Merton, Parsons working at the macro- and microlevels (Parsons 1951; Parsons and Shils 1951); and Merton (1957) at the middle level. Political scientists recognized three forms of functionalism— 'eclectic,' 'empirical,' and structural-functionalism (Flanagan and Fogelman 1967, 72–75)—and tended to adopt the latter as the most important innovation (Bill and Hardgrave 1973, 201–17).

The Politics of the Developing Areas (Almond and Coleman 1960) represented the early culmination of structural-functionalism in political science (Bill and Hardgrave 1973, 212–13), after which structural-functionalism divided into two not altogether parallel paths. The work of Almond and Powell (1966) was designed to give focus to the Little, Brown series of comparative politics texts, and used several types of functions: 'capability' functions (regulative, extractive, distributive, and responsive); 'conversion' functions (the original input and output functions such as interest aggregation, rule making, and so on); and 'maintenance and adaptation' functions (socialization and recruitment).

The second path, represented eventually by the authors of the Binder volume, considered itself to be working in the same structural-functional tradition (Binder's introduction states this explicitly; Binder et al. 1971, 27), but it redirected attention to the 'crises' that disrupted the static functional order. The six volumes that preceded the Binder synthesis stemmed from the original Almond and Coleman book, under the direction of the Committee on Comparative Politics of the Social Science Research Council. According to a recent commentator, the volumes were "highly touted" but of marginal impact on research in the comparative field (Migdal 1983, 310).

In a recent oral history, Almond has emphasized that the institutional background of the series was not always sufficient to cause the contributing authors to follow the framework, and that the framework itself did not intuitively recommend itself to them (Baer, Jewell, and Sigelman 1991, 132). This was the reason the Binder volume was awaited with such interest, and why the blanket criticism by Holt and Turner in the *American Political Science Review* was so definitive. The functional framework itself, independent of its use in political science, was subject to widespread criticism; see, for instance, Finer (1969–70), Groth (1970), Hempel (1959).

The decline of interest in structural-functionalism was in part associated with a secular decline in 'development theory' as social and political change came to seem far more difficult in pace and direction than originally anticipated. But the loss of structural-functionalism as a dynamic theoretical force within comparative politics was also a response to a specific failure—the failure of an 'approach' to transform itself into an at least partially formalized 'theory.'

Theory and Criticism

The challenge to make structural-functionalism into a political theory was issued by Sidney Verba in the final chapter of the *Crises and Sequences in Political Development* volume (Binder et al. 1971), which climaxed the political science portion of the Social Science Research Council's comparative politics project of the period.[2] Critics would later roundly condemn the project for its failure to fulfill that challenge (Holt and Turner 1975). Whatever the cause, however, structural-functionalism soon joined the history of comparative politics rather than its present. Hindsight suggests this may have been a premature burial.

The question is a vital one because of the high investment made by the comparative politics field in the structural-functional movement in terms of time, resources, and hopes. "The promise of structural functionalism is nothing less than to provide a consistent and integrated theory from which can be derived explanatory hypotheses relevant to all aspects of a political system," according to one early account (Flanagan and Fogelman 1967, 76). Others were more cautious (Bill and Hardgrave 1973; Holt and Turner 1970), but everyone gave it a predominant place in their discussions. Its fall therefore is of major interest to the field (Migdal 1983, 310).

I make here the basic argument that structural-functionalism in political science was in fact closer to the achievement of true theoretical status than it seemed to observers in the 1970s. Reconsideration after a score of years suggests that many if not all the ideas behind the structural-functional movement could have been recast into a form that would have satisfied the critics' strictures against vagueness and ambiguity in the original approach.

The present inquiry can begin with the challenge issued by Verba (1971), which formed the concluding chapter to that work. The text deserves full quotation even after twenty years.

> Speculation about the consequences of alternative sequences among the five problem areas and about the consequences of a cumulative pattern of crises or problems illustrates the usefulness of such an approach to the study of political development. If we could convert these speculations into testable hypotheses, we might have a powerful tool indeed for dealing with developmental histories in comparative perspective. Furthermore, such an approach might produce findings of great relevance to those interested in applying the findings of developmental studies to policy choice situations. . . .
>
> But the usefulness of such studies of developmental patterns based on hypotheses about alternative orderings of the problems of crises and the consequences of such orderings should also underscore the need for furthering [sic] 'processing' of the 'five crises' model of development for the purpose of further studies. . . . It is hoped that the potential usefulness of this approach to development will lead to attempts to deal with the more difficult task of converting the 'five crises scheme' into a more precise model of political development. Until the processing is done, discussion . . . may remain quite vague. (Verba 1971, 316)

Critics would several years later raise the same issues, charging that without some formalization, "seventeen years of prodigious effort" were set at naught (Holt and Turner 1975, 988).

Varieties of Functionalism

The prospect of turning the 'approach' into a 'theory' seemed therefore unpromising. Structural-functionalism seemed to imply theory about social wholes *as* social wholes (Parsons 1951), but critics had attacked all the holistic conceptual apparatus associated with structural-functionalism as ambiguous and an inadequate base for operational theory (e.g., Hempel 1959). It was overlooked by political scientists that structural-functionalism contained within itself a second methodology based on microanalytic, individualistic postulates (Parsons and Shils 1951). This oversight perhaps occurred because the individualistic methodology was thought to be associated only with rational-choice theories, perhaps because any sort of actor-centered theory seemed too distant from the aggregates with which comparative politics students needed to concern themselves—states and other national groupings.[3]

Decision-making theories are very plausible, but for anyone wishing to deal with large political aggregates, the amount of detail involved seems overwhelming. Yet some theorists have shown that carefully constructed models can be based on individual choice formulas, while serving to explain aggregate behavior. Bates (1981), for instance, showed that 'failures' in national development were explicable if one understood the political environment within which peasants made agricultural decisions. North and Thomas (1973), using a similar strategy, explained 'the rise of the Western world' in terms of negotiations between elite political actors over taxes and financial arrangements (see Chapter 2).

These works serve as a reminder that 'process theories' of the sort the *Crises and Sequences* authors advocated can be developed at the microanalytic level without necessarily overwhelming the conceptual wagon. This recognition leads to the major 'correction' needed to turn the structural-functional-crisis approach into a specifiable model of political behavior: the standing of structural-functionalism "on its head," in other words, recasting it as microanalytic theory rather than macroanalysis.

As the term 'correction' suggests, the present chapter takes a radical, although respectful, approach to the original framework summarized in the Binder-edited volume (1971). Rather than accepting wholesale the structural-functional approach as presented by the several authors of that work, it is recast in a different mode, one that appears to display it in a more acceptably scientific form. That is to say, the structural-functional approach is not allowed to present itself in its own way; rather, the contributors are challenged to answer questions suggested by a formal theory, questions that the structural-functional theorists would not themselves have asked. Such a strategy can be justified only by the degree to which the clarification provides a suitable model for the analysis of comparative and developmental problems.

To preview the results of this analysis, it may be said (1) that structural-functionalism stands up well to the challenge presented, answering the necessary questions directly and firmly; (2) that the derived structural-functional model is of wider scope than the original model; (3) that 'development' becomes less likely, from the new viewpoint; and (4) that the revised structural-functional model is equivalent to the politics model.

The *Crises and Sequences* Contributors

Because the standing of anything on its head is presumptuous at best, the perpetrator must show, first, that the authors of the original framework give some sanction to the procedure. In the present section, therefore, the several chapters of the *Crises and Sequences* volume (Binder et al. 1971) are consulted in light of the possibility that their actual understanding of structural-functionalism was not wholly coincident with the terms in which it was presented. Because the Binder collection has a high degree of unity despite being written by several authors, it is natural to take the chapters in order, with each contributing a phase of an integrated argument.

The flagship chapter by James C. Coleman presents the structural-functional approach in the form for which it was best known, a dialectical interpretation of macroconcepts such as differentiation, integration, and so on. Succeeding chapters fluctuated in their viewpoint: Some concepts, such as national 'identity' and 'participation,' brought out the strongest bent toward the microperspective; other concepts, such as legitimacy and penetration, made the microanalytic perspective difficult to employ.

Coleman's Chapter 2 defines political development in terms of three concepts: a "continuous interaction among the processes of structural *differentiation*, the imperatives of *equality*, and the integrative, responsive and adaptive *capacity* of a political system" (Coleman 1971, 74).

Political development, in these terms, is seen as the acquisition by a political system of a consciously sought, and a qualitatively new and enhanced political capacity as manifested in the successful institutional-ization of (1) new patterns of *integration* and *penetration* regulating and containing the tensions and conflicts produced by increased differentia-tion, and (2) new patterns of *participation* and resource *distribution* adequately responsive to the demands generated by the imperatives of equality. The acquisition of such a performance capacity is, in turn, a decisive factor in the resolution of the problems of *identity* and *legiti-macy*. (Coleman 1971, 74–75)

This admirable summary of the ideas in which structural-functionalism culminated is notable not only for its breathtakingly high level of gen-eralization but for its apparent inconsistency with its own claim, in the paragraph just preceding, that structural-functionalism will 'liberate' the concept of political development from its Western bias, and "en-compass the full range of cultural diversity" in human government (Coleman 1971, 74). The framework presented seems, in hindsight, a transparently Western model and an idealized model as well.

Empirical Questions

Differentiation processes are defined by Coleman, in reference to the political system, as "progressive separation and specialization of roles, institutional spheres, and associations," leading to an increasing num-ber of "explicit and functionally specific administrative and political structures" (1971, 72). *Equality* includes national citizenship, a uni-versalistic legal order, and achievement norms. Finally, *capacity* is defined as the ability to manage the tensions created by the other elements, and a growing ability to formulate and achieve new goals. Coleman then presents the integrating hypothesis, that "as a polity develops or modernizes (increases in differentiation, equality and ca-pacity) certain crises are generated: identity, legitimacy, participation, penetration, and distribution" (1971, 73).

Since this hypothesis is the central pivot upon which the theory balances, it is important that it be logically firm and empirically direct. Holt and Turner (1975) level three criticisms against it: tautology, vagueness, and nonoperationalizability. The tautology inheres in the three basic definitions, where capacity and differentiation are interlinked, as indeed is equality, which, as defined by Coleman, includes citizenship differentiation and mass political capacity. The research criticisms—vagueness and nonmeasurability—supplement the logical criticisms: If the researcher cannot measure the basic concepts, then they cannot be used to test specific hypotheses.

The basic crisis-sequence concepts may be attacked on other grounds as well. Where, for instance, do the processes, imperatives, and capacities originate? Coleman refers to the 'imperatives' of equality, but unless we resort to Hegel's *weltgeist* there is no source of imperatives except individual actors. 'Capacities' seem similarly disembodied in the model. Can the capacity of, say, the agricultural marketing commissions be distinguished from the goals and capacities of the relevant employees? The crisis-sequence contributors might respond, however, that only a very blockheaded critic would raise such questions. 'Obviously,' they might say, 'we knew there were people at the base of the whole edifice, but they were not our concern: we sought systemwide concepts and universal correlations.

But to make a theory operational, lines must be drawn from theory to real political worlds. To say that equality rises as a disembodied 'imperative' is vague and insufficient. A more defensible explanation would be that the imperative of equality occurs when certain political actors seeking leadership of certain political groups adopt specific claims (equal protection under law, for instance) that they think will cause people to rally to them. Such a microanalytic, 'upended' perspective defines development in terms of what kinds of groups and leaders are making what kinds of demands on the formal government leaders. This microanalytic model also sensitizes us (as structural-functionalism did not always so sensitize us) to recognize that some, perhaps all, groups are demanding not equality but inequality—special privileges for themselves and their associates.

Political Identity

The microanalytic interpretation of structural-functionalism taken by the authors who succeeded Coleman in the Binder (1971) volume frequently presents a striking contrast to his initial formulation. Pye's chapter on political identity (1971, 101–34) is based directly on the activity of elites with different types of motivation in respect to mass inclusion in the political system. Six forms of elite political culture are defined (expansive, exclusive, closed, parochial, synthetic, and null), and though no similar classification of mass attitudes is included, the importance of specific mass–elite political controversies is implicit in the attention Pye gives to socialization processes and their relation to political legitimacy. As Pye notes:

> Although in our discussion of the four general types of identity crises that revolve around orientation toward territory, class, ethnicity, and time or social change we have mentioned the conditions that might be conducive to the resolution of each type of crisis, it should be apparent that precisely because identity involves the search for a sense of uniqueness, it is peculiarly difficult to arrive at any generalizations about the essential character of a resolved identity crisis. Much depends upon the particular issues in the crisis and the substantive character of the specific cultures involved. (1971, 123–24)

Pye briefly considers specific stratagems for countering identity problems, but shortly shifts to a 'middle-range' theory connecting the type of political elite culture to chosen political strategies. An 'inclusive' elite will, for instance, accommodate a new class if the new class accepts "the essential spirit of the dominant political culture" as in Anglo-American historical experience (1971, 124–25). A 'parochial' elite, on the other hand, will ban certain groups from participation (1971, 129–31). Pye thus virtually abandons the abstract concept of 'identity' in favor of a detailed analysis of specific types of political controversy.

In his second chapter, on the crisis of legitimacy, Pye maintains his emphasis on the politics underlying the structural-functional concepts, rather than utilize the concepts in their abstract purity. It is true that Pye freely mixes the two vocabularies. On the one hand he uses such 'orthodox' structural-functional formulation as: "[A]ll advances in the developmental syndrome, with any concomitant changes in the relationships among equality, capacity and differentiation, are likely to produce reactions that affect legitimacy and can bring on a major crisis" (1971, 135–36). On the other hand, however, and fully in accord with the microanalytic approach suggested in this chapter, Pye notes that "the acknowledgment of legitimacy resides with the people" and exists only when they are satisfied in practical political terms (1971, 135).

Pye's four explanations of legitimacy crises are largely cast in concrete terms: Crises occur, that is, when the elite cannot find grounds for its claims of authority, when the elite is splintered and a 'raw' power struggle ensues, when elite promises fail to be achieved, and when the people are difficult to please because they have not been sufficiently socialized in the norms of deference to authority (1971, 139–46). These eminently "concrete" definitions of ideas that various critics of structural-functionalism have condemned as ambiguous and abstract are reinforced by Pye's conclusion that psychology and anthropology must be used to understand the basic political 'process' that underlies the legitimacy concept (1971, 146). His succeeding discussion of the practical problems of interaction between elites and masses reinforce this point. Development is no longer an inevitable movement of broad forces, but a tricky process during which, for instance, leaders must convince followers "to make sacrifices for goals unrelated to their immediate wishes" and must avoid being thrown out of office as a result of citizen anger (1971, 154).

Political Participation

Myron Weiner's chapter on participation (1971, 159–204) is among the Binder volume's most 'operational' analyses of the structural-functional concepts involved in the development process. It neatly complements Pye's chapters on identity and legitimacy. Where Pye concerns himself primarily with elite responses to mass pressures, Weiner categorizes these mass demands and strategies, and then summarizes the entire process by indicating what the outcomes of mass demand and elite response patterns will be. The framework in which the structural-functional hypotheses would be cast, in light of the Pye and Weiner approaches, is simple:

Demands of type 'x' made by mass publics, and
Responses of type 'y' by governing and other elites,
Result in a political outcome (sometimes a crisis) of type 'z.'

Weiner's chapter is devoted to putting empirical flesh on this basic skeleton.

The foundation of Weiner's participation model is that socioeconomic conditions or patterns create occupation-status-income categories; for instance, new technology may create new occupational categories. These various occupational categories determine expectations in respect to 'power' and participation, and thereby influence the demands a group will make. Because socioeconomic conditions change often, the occupational categories and thus the demands change; and the result is that participation crises tend to recur, not occur once only (1971, 203). The demands are classified by Weiner into 'moderate' and 'extreme' in respect to the manner of their presentation; and classified in respect to their content into 'legitimate' and 'illegitimate,' with legitimate defined as a decision to "work within the existing legal framework set by government authority."

These definitions are followed by an empirical generalization that moderate, legitimate demands win support from outside, usually governmental, elites, while the same demands lose support of militants within the demanding group's own membership. Conversely, extreme demands solidify loyalty within the group, but may provoke repression by governmental elites (1971, 201–2). The quality of the group's demands influences also the ability to form coalitions with other groups to increase their bargaining strength, or alternatively "maintaining purity of purpose."

Political Institutionalization

The response of elites to mass demands is defined by Weiner in a manner that is simpler than Pye's solution discussed above, but it is not incompatible with that earlier formulation. In an interesting equation, Weiner refers to "political systems or, more precisely, governing elites" (1971, 192) and observes that demand characteristics influence response characteristics. That is to say, for instance, that a rapid rise in demands may frighten elites, and a crisis will likely ensue; elites respond with repression. This occurs perhaps when the demands exceed available financial and administrative resources (1971, 193).

A major element in building an operational model of structural-functionalism is employed by Weiner in discussing elite behavior: the hypothesis, so often denied by 'rationality' theorists, that elites in different systems make varying responses to the same demands. This affirms a cultural-cognitive variance and represents a belief that comparativists have often held in defiance of their 'economic' colleagues (1971, 193). Some elites will be willing to 'share' power; some will not. Some will admit new groups into political participation, others will not. This receptivity to outside demands is effectively manifested by the creation of new institutions such as new electoral procedures, new parties, new interest groups (1971, 193). If institutions do work, do offer "a reasonable chance of satisfying" the demands of the new groups, the institutions become legitimate, offering rewards for those who use them. If use of the institutions is not satisfactory, on the other hand, they will disappear (1971, 193).

The results of these interactive processes fall into three categories: the democratic, the authoritarian, and the 'encapsulation' outcomes. The democratic response, for instance, occurs when the crisis is resolved through the agreement of governing and contending elites and political participants on "the legitimacy of demands and on the value of certain institutional procedures created to meet the demands." The working class may win the right to organize and strike, for example, in return for working within institutional rules (1971, 194). That this model is process-oriented, concrete, and dynamic is illustrated by Weiner's statement that, in such interactions, nothing is permanently settled: "No institutional settlement is ever necessarily final" (1971, 195).

The open-negotiation quality of this 'upended' model is illustrated, to take another case, in Weiner's analysis of the way in which new regimes are able to suppress opposition but unable to enforce compliance "upon a predominantly illiterate, nonindustrial, rural population." The elites therefore create a new strategy, encouraging citizens to support the regime "without allowing them to make any demands upon it" (1971, 198; the reference is to Pakistan in 1956).

This flexible, fluid, highly open-ended model is summarized in Weiner's process-based, 'political' definition of participation:

> . . . I shall use the concept of political participation to refer to any voluntary action, successful or unsuccessful, organized or unorganized, episodic or continuous, employing legitimate or illegitimate methods intended to influence the choice of public policies, the administration of public affairs, or the choice of political leaders at any level of government, local or national. (1971, 164)

The strictures usually directed against structural-functionalism are simply inappropriate when the framework is inverted and defined in such dynamic politically interactive terms.[4]

Penetration and Distribution

LaPalombara's two chapters, on penetration and distribution, which conclude the basic presentation in the Binder volume (1971), are on the surface the most traditionally developmental, emphasizing problems of elite capacity, steering, and control at a high level of generalization. But this apparently traditional mode is deceptive. In fact, LaPalombara's analysis is vigorously political and bereft of all of structural-functionalism's hopeful illusions about development; instead a hard-edged competitive model emerges.

Penetration refers not to the benign direction of modernizing leaders, but to the bald question of whether political elites "can get what they want from people over whom they seek to exercise power" (1971, 209).

> It is easier to mobilize . . . than to permit participation; easier to coerce than seek to induce; easier to silence opposition by force than to permit it relatively free reign [*sic*] in suggesting policy alternatives . . . ; easier . . . to assume that in politics, as in all of life, the other man's gain is one's personal loss. (1971, 278)

This final reduction of structural-functionalism's hopeful attitudes about development to, at the end of the scale, the contemplation of harsh political realities sets the stage for Verba's concluding chapter.[5]

Criticism from Within

The chapter by Sidney Verba, which concludes the *Crises and Sequences* volume (Binder et al. 1971), is faithful in its attempted adherence to the structural-functional framework, judicious in evaluation of the framework's strengths and weaknesses, original in the search for increased theoretical rigor—and ultimately devastating in its criticism. The 'crises,' Verba argues, are ill-defined and are, at most, mere problem areas (1971, 299, 302). In respect to the 'sequences,' there are none (1971, 300); and if there were, the definitions are so vague that one might not be able to recognize them (1971, 309). The theory is but a framework (1971, 283, 286). The defined list of crises is neither exhaustive nor mutually exclusive (1971, 306). There is no necessary movement through the crises to greater political capacity (1971, 312). The relationships among demands, performance, and institutionalization are 'abstract,' 'vague,' and 'not clear' (1971, 313).

Yet this is far from the whole story. Verba's chapter has the same dualism that has been noted in reference to earlier chapters in the Binder volume; concrete empirical interpretations are interspersed with generalized, often vague structural-functional ideas. What makes Verba's chapter distinctive, however, is his maintenance of a demand that the theory should fulfill the criteria of scientific research, the development and testing of operational hypotheses. "If we could convert these speculations [about political development] into testable hypotheses, we might have a powerful tool indeed for dealing with developmental histories in comparative perspective" (1971, 316). This ends in pessimism: The 'five crises' model will not be useful, Verba argues in the passage quoted earlier, until further 'processing' is completed, and "until that processing is done, the discussion of sequence— as exemplified, I am afraid, by the present chapter—may remain quite vague" (1971, 316).

Yet this is unduly dismissive of the contributions made by Verba himself and the other Binder contributors at the practical level of research-oriented theory. Some of these contributions have been discussed above. It is now time to gather them into a tentative body of actual propositions, which might form the beginning of an 'upended' structural-functional theory.

A Microperspective on Structural-Functionalism

In the process of turning a 'framework' into a theory, one wants first to locate the axioms or assumptions on which the theory depends—those elements of commonality, that is to say, that are fundamental premises for the theory. After having laid this infrastructure, specific hypotheses relating to real world behavior may be added. This section deals with the basic axiomatic structure; hypotheses, empirical generalizations and specific definitions are presented in the next section.

The results of putting structural-functional theory into a politics model can be summarized in four points, which define the basic theoretic premises of the approach revised in the manner proposed here. The outline follows directly from Verba's description of the theoretical course he thought structural-functionalism should take (1971, 305). In the place of excessively large generalizations about whole systems, the microanalytic approach defines *who* engages in politics, *what* they demand, and *how* the resulting controversy is brought to resolution or nonresolution. Such an approach to analysis, as I have shown in earlier chapters, is by no means unfamiliar to political scientists. What is somewhat unexpected, however, is the possibility that the politics model has the capacity to serve as a foundation for structural-functional theory.

The empirical model of structural-functionalism is based on several axioms or postulates that lay out the scope and presuppositions of the model. These postulates involve (1) the definition of the actors, (2) the goals of the actors, (3) the cognitive nature of the actors, and (4) the nature of the interrelationship between the participants.

Groups of Actors

1. How are actors defined?   The actors are defined as groups rather than individuals. Most frequently the terms are 'elites,' 'masses,' 'the government.' (Occasionally an individual actor may enter the picture, usually as the leader of a nation or a competitor elite.)

The first proposition redefines the theory of structural-functionalism in microanalytic rather than macroanalytic terms. It may seem a surprising change to those who are accustomed to viewing structural-functionalism as holistic theory, but the Binder authors' analyses discussed above confirm that such a model underlies much of the discussion in that volume. In every chapter the exposition proceeds in terms of elite and other group interests. Pye's chapter is notable in this regard, for he defines a wide variety of national developmental outcomes largely in terms of the strategies pursued by the elite actors—to include or exclude other groups, to share or not to share values.

The notion of 'capacity' in Coleman's chapter is rooted in the same group-based perspective, although in the style of the time, references are usually to the capacity of the whole polity. But this attribution of capacity to the whole is merely shorthand for saying that elites, usually governmental elites, either do or do not make their decisions well, i.e. in a manner satisfactory to the other actors. 'Penetration' is similarly better understood at the microanalytic level. Political systems do not penetrate themselves, as macroanalytic terminology seems vaguely to suggest. Rather, penetration means that the government (one group) gets the mass (another group or groups) to obey its strictures and laws.

Multiple Definitions of Self-Interest

2. What are the actors' goals?   The actors are self-interested but will vary in how they define that self-interest (e.g., Pye's elites); socialization is a major factor in establishing goals. (It is important to note the commitment to different goals; no implicit preconceptions narrow the range of choice.)

In the second of the four propositions, structural-functionalism makes perhaps its most characteristic statement. Throughout the volume, the authors implicitly assume that self-interest, both in elites and masses, may take many forms; or, in other words, self-interest may define different goals for different people. Pye particularly emphasizes this aspect, as one might expect in light of his interest in political culture. Pye postulates that elites behave differently in different countries and circumstances: Some elites share norms and rewards with the masses, other elites shut out one or more subgroups; some elites modernize, some sell out to foreign influences (1971, 124–33). Masses, too, vary in their motivations, and the interaction between elites and masses becomes therefore characteristic of the particular mix of groups and goals in a given situation (Weiner 1971, 175–82; LaPalombara 1971, 223). As Verba later suggests, Disraeli could extend voting rights because he assumed, correctly, that the people were sufficiently docile that it would not be dangerous (1971, 315).

The emphasis in structural-functionalism on the processes of socialization is also testimony to this cultural diversity of motives. It is difficult for a leader always to supply citizens with the actual goods they seek; it is easier to instill somehow a loyalty based on symbolic or cultural goods. That some peoples might prefer national 'purity,' for instance, rather than fast economic development has always seemed inconvenient for rational-choice theory—but it accords easily with the structural-functional model constructed here.[6]

Cognitive Variation among Actors

3. How do the actors pursue their goals?   The actors, rather than being abstractly 'rational,' will vary in their cognitive characteristics according to the group's cultural norms.

The third structural-functional postulate, that there is not only goal variance but pervasive cognitive variance among acting groups, is implicit in Verba's statement that "[d]ifferent actors in a situation will define a problem differently" (1971, 306). Such variation involves more than Simon's notion of bounded rationality, which implies the imperfection of cognitive resources and skills in most human decision makers (Kahneman, Slovic, and Tversky 1982). Cognitive variance in a cross-national perspective opens to research investigation the whole field suggested by Wittgenstein's language games, each of which is complete and correct 'in its own way'; or the kind of cognitive differences studied by Levi-Strauss (1966) or Foucault (1973).

Rational-choice theorists frequently claim to hold the same position here as do the structural-functionalists, emphasizing diversity of response to similar stimuli; yet their diversity is a narrow-range diversity, a sort of American middle-class twentieth-century diversity. Structural-functionalists such as those included in the Binder volume have not attended fully to the issue; nor, for that matter, have sociologists, presumably in the belief that the division of labor leaves such matter to cognitive psychologists. But it must be recalled that 'political culture' has a place in contemporary comparative politics largely because it was introduced and maintained by structural-functionalists, including such major figures as Gabriel Almond and Lucien Pye.

Complex Political Interaction

4. What is the relation among actors?   Interaction among the actor groups deals with "the problems of allocations of resources among competing interests, each with some political power and political resources" (Verba 1971, 312).

The fourth and final proposition defines interaction not as exchange (where everyone is said to benefit), nor as war (where payoffs are often zero-sum), but as ongoing competitive struggle among different types of actors with varying cognitions, goals, and resources. In other words, structural-functional 'forces' disappear, and only interactive, multidirectional politics remains. From this point on, the structural-functional model must be composed of hypotheses defining what will happen when one group (with stated goals and defined resources) meets other groups (with equally diverse goals, cognitions, and resources). The resulting outcomes would include such standard terms as strengthened legitimacy, widened participation, increased equality and capacity (or, conversely, weakened legitimacy, narrowed participation, and so on).

That this fourth postulate may seem merely to mirror rational-choice theory serves as the occasion to reemphasize differences of scope, complexity, and outcome between the two approaches. Rational-choice theory usually emphasizes only one kind of resource—money or, say, the military might that money can buy. Structural-functionalism provides, on the contrary, space for motives of duty, nationalism, and a whole gamut of other motivations. A further difference is that rational-choice theory gives almost no attention to the context of the interaction; instead the context is postulated a priori. (Hayward Alker has been asking for years whether, in the Prisoner's Dilemma, it might not be interesting to find out more about the sheriff and the specific crime.) Structural-functionalism escapes this focus on an isolated point of interaction because the whole thrust of its program requires it to investigate and understand the background of events.

One further major background difference between the two schools is that rational-choice theorists have a constant interest in discovering social equilibria, those points where actors and events have settled into stability. Structural-functionalism studies interactions from a quite contrary perspective, that of change, development, modernization, and, in general, 'politics' of all sorts. Though the language may seem the same, substantial differences exist between the structural-functional model presented here and any current forms of rational-choice theory.

If, as Holt and Turner argued, structural-functionalism's goal was "a theory of political development based upon a conceptualization of the whole political process changing through time" (Holt and Turner 1975, 980), then the Binder volume was a success in providing the materials for such a theory. It also provided an array of specific hypotheses, to which it is now appropriate to turn as a way of demonstrating that the theory is not just a framework but has substantive content.

Explanations and Predictions

As a way of visualizing the model's conceptual precision, as well as its theoretical incompleteness, it is useful to imagine a matrix, with the various types of elites across the top and the various types of mass groups at the left side. The cells would then be filled with the 'outcome' when a particular type of elite faced a particular type of social group. When, for example, a weak government elite with no resources faces a radically conservative group of landowners, then there will occur what structural-functionalism would have called a penetration crisis (a defeat of the government). Or when a strong competent elite faces a famine-ridden peasantry and delivers the required food, then a distribution crisis is avoided, and legitimacy levels are increased. Though the task of filling in the cells seems large, nonetheless structural-functionalism has defined the task correctly, and this is no small achievement.

In order to maintain a close connection with the actual presentation of the authors of the Binder volume, the definitions and hypotheses presented below are grouped according to the author, rather than summarizing the whole book in a single anonymous framework. Because of the division of labor the authors observed, this procedure retains identifiability without substantially affecting the coherence.

Pye's chapter on 'identity' crises begins with the postulate that in every political system, two groups exist: an elite group made up of governmental and nongovernmental leaders, and a mass or citizen group. Each group has a distinctive political culture; the masses may have several political cultures, based on class, region, ethnicity, and similar factors. The elite political culture includes attitudes on leadership norms and on effective policy formulation; the mass political cultures include values that relate to democratic cooperation (Pye 1971, 103).

> *Proposition:* Where the elite and mass orientations are 'compatible' (but not necessarily homogeneous), then the outcome will be stability; where the elite is competent (i.e., responsive), the masses will reduce their opposition to its control (Pye 1971, 103, 133–34).
>
> *Proposition:* Where the elite and mass cultures clash because the elite makes unacceptable demands, then there will be a legitimacy crisis; if the clash raises questions about basic social unity, then this is an identity crisis (Pye 1971, 104).
>
> *Proposition:* Political cultures are formed by conditions in the economy and society, the level of technology, and communications levels (Pye 1971, 104).
>
> *Proposition:* Where elites cannot meet, or they fail to meet, international development models, then the masses will challenge the elite (Pye 1971, 105).
>
> *Proposition:* If economic and technological changes are abrupt, then

there will result deep divisions between elite and mass political cultures (Pye 1971, 106).

Proposition: Elites and masses may have several types of goals: emotional nationalism, civil service careers, traditional power and status, personal power, public service (Pye 1971, 106–7).

Proposition: Under some (unstated) conditions, cleavages result in overthrow of the old authorities; under other (similarly unspecified) conditions, there will be mass–elite accommodation (Pye 1971, 107–8).

Proposition: Some leaders and followers (who are not further identified) are prone to unrealistic behavior, verbiage, and slogans; others make realistic appraisals and plans; where idealism fails, some will deny the failure, others attack those believed to be at fault (Pye 1971, 108–9).

Proposition: Leaders who employ traditional leadership ideas (involving status, dignity, aloofness) are more apt to fail than those who are aggressively involved in problem solving (Pye 1971, 109).

Proposition: Where elites produce 'visible benefits' for masses, 'identity' is increased; where groups benefit differentially, the elites will be challenged by those groups who feel they are not sufficiently benefited (Pye 1971, 115, 117).

Proposition: Leaders who invest heavily in, say, education, may escape identity crises (challenges to their rule) (Pye 1971, 124).

Proposition: There are several types of elite cultures, each characterized by a specific type of response to mass demands: Leaders with an 'expanding' political culture will distribute some goods to all citizens, leaders with an 'exclusive' political culture will exclude significant groups from benefits, leaders with 'closed' political cultures will benefit only themselves, leaders with 'parochial' cultures will shut out other elites. Finally, where there is no national elite, a many-sided controversy will ensue (Pye 1971, 124–33).

Pye's Chapter 4 on 'legitimacy' focuses further on the relations between elites and mass actors, particularly emphasizing the notion of mass 'alienation,' which he describes as the actual problem underlying the crises of legitimacy and identity (Pye 1971, 157). Pye begins with several definitions, each of which emphasizes the operational aspect of structural-functional categories.

Proposition: Legitimacy is the process by which a society decides "what particular structures shall be considered to be the authoritative ones" (Pye 1971, 135).

Proposition: "The acknowledgement of legitimacy resides with the people" (Pye 1971, 135).

Proposition: Legitimacy crises occur when there is disagreement about the "proper nature of authority" in the system; but because this is very wide, the term *legitimacy* will be restricted to "breakdown in the constitutional basis of government" (Pye 1971, 136–37).

There are four principal hypotheses presented in the chapter. The consequent of the propositions is the same in each case: The term Pye has substituted for the two crises is alienation. The antecedents of the propositions state the causes of increasing this alienation.

1. If leaders are unable "to find a popularly acceptable rationale" for their authority, then alienation will increase.
2. If there are too many elites contending for power in the absence of institutions, then alienation will increase.
3. If elites use ideologies that are unacceptable to the masses, or if the elites fail to meet their promises, then alienation will increase.
4. If the masses have not been socialized to revere authority, then (presumably when elite planning fails) alienation will increase. This final hypothesis is, according to Pye, the "most fundamental" reason for failure.

Pye at this point advocates Eckstein's theory of authority congruence and suggests the need to combine cultural beliefs, religious ideas, social practices, and leadership styles in the effort further to understand these processes (Pye 1971, 138–46).

A Model of Participation

Weiner's chapter on participation follows from and supplements Pye's discussion. Weiner puts his emphasis on elite behavior, as did Pye, but his fine definition of participation, cited above, gives a generous definition of the demands made by the populace (Weiner 1971, 164). He provides several hypotheses in relation to the existence of mass demands.

> *Proposition:* If (1) urbanization and mobilization increase, (2) social stratification changes occur, (3) intellectuals are in conflict and employ ideologies as weapons, and (4) exposure to government demands occurs, then the affected groups will increase their demands (Weiner 1971, 166–75; see also 202–4).

A further set of propositions fills out the linkage of variables begun by Pye. Where Pye explained how various sorts of elites might behave in respect to mass demands, Weiner takes the chain further, to integrate elite–mass challenge and response into the development of new institutional forms. Two possible outcomes are defined: first, crisis; second "orderly institutional adaptation" (Weiner 1971, 193).

> *Proposition:* Orderly institutional adaptation occurs "when there is a new agreement among governing elites, contending elites, and political participants on the legitimacy of demands and on the value of certain institutional procedures created to meet the demands" (Weiner 1971, 194). Several illustrations show this process as one of exchange—a group is given a right to do something, and in return it agrees, say, to follow legal guidelines.

The elite responses are defined by Weiner in institutional terms rather than in Pye's political-cultural terms.

> *Proposition:* The elite may reject the people's demands if (1) the elite does not approve of the group making the demand, (2) the elite disapproves of the methods used to make the demands, or (3) the demands involve policies that are outside the range defined as acceptable by the elite (independence, for instance) (Weiner 1971, 187–92).

The Need for Specificity

Much of LaPalombara's treatment of the penetration and distribution crises is at the high level of generalization associated with macro-analytic structural-functionalism, rather than at the operational level of the microanalytic model sought here. Careful search discloses a number of specific propositions, however. In discussing the penetration crisis, LaPalombara emphasizes that the level of technology is not a central factor; developed nations such as Canada have problems similar to those of underdeveloped nations (LaPalombara 1971, 208, 210, 212–13). Some undefined goal or attribute such as 'modernity' cannot therefore make the penetration problem a technical one; LaPalombara's emphasis is on the interpersonal or sociopolitical aspects rather than the physical circumstances.

What policies do elites seek to impose on the people, and what groups protest those policies to what degree? These are LaPalombara's basic unifying questions. This is shown in his definition of penetration: ". . . [F]or any elite, penetration refers to whether they can get what they want from people over whom they seek to exercise power." Conversely, at the mass level (or, as LaPalombara generally phrases it, the "objects of policy"), penetration is a matter of the "predisposition . . . to receive information . . . and to wish to conform to such policies voluntarily" (1971, 209). LaPalombara's axiomatic basis therefore involves the "social-psychological structures" that predispose elites and masses to choose their own strategies (1971, 211). He suggests three elite categories, without elaborating them fully—nation builders, centralizers, and crisis managers—and is probably referring to more or less distinct types of roles that elite actors may choose or have thrust upon them (1971, 212). Subelites include "political parties, armies, clubs, bureaucracies, etc.," who also focus on the citizens (1971, 217). There are apparently three basic citizen roles: to demand a policy, to accept a policy, or to resist (1971, 211, 217, 223).

These several levels of actors are included in a general process, as a result of which new organizations and institutions may be created (1971, 218). That the specific hypotheses are not worked out in detail is a result of LaPalombara's reticence about the macrolevel of analysis at which the book is intended to be couched. He remarks, for instance, that "generalizations alone about meeting the crisis of penetration with *specific* patterns of organization will simply not do," and he advocates a policy very close to the argument of the present essay: that "profiles" of specific nations be prepared before hypotheses are advanced. Such profiles would certainly include analyses of a nation's social groups, elites, leaders, and the kind of concrete specification of circumstances used in an operationally defined model (1971, 228–30). While a few hypotheses are suggested, such as the importance of military groups in "empty territories" crises, specialized civil servants for peasant crises, etc., overall he devotes much of the discussion to the hopes for modernization and national development that were current at the time.[7]

Collecting the Theory

As the exhausted reader will have observed, a collection of rough hypotheses liberally mixed with empirical generalizations does not constitute a coherent theory. In conclusion one must ask if a logically integrated model can be developed on the basis of the Binder volume's several contributors. Here recourse to Verba's final chapter is appropriate.

Because of its origins as an internal memorandum for the Committee on Comparative Politics, directed specifically to the "crisis-sequence" schema, Verba's chapter does not transcend the framework; nor did he intend it to do so. Yet in the midst of his highly critical discussion, Verba provides the key that becomes central to the present attempt to operationalize structural-functionalism. That key was simply the idea of institutions, which "are created to handle problems in each problem area." More important than formal institutions are informal ones, defined as "generally accepted regular procedures for handling a problem" and "normatively sanctioned behavior patterns."[8]

Institutions might include a national administrative service, agreements on language issues and education, the franchise, mass political parties, the tax system (Verba 1971, 300). Institutionalization, Verba notes, comes "very close to the third dimension of the developmental triad—differentiation" and is a major part of the process of innovation and government responsiveness, which is the main structural-functional focus (Verba 1971, 301).

Verba's use of institutionalization is multidirectional: Institutionalization includes not only changes that result in a system's greater capacity, but also the "collapse" of existing institutions or whole governments (303). From this perspective, attention can be directed toward the environmental changes that stimulate new demands, mass–elite relations, elite imbalances, and other interactions between relevant actors (304–5). Verba also remarks on the contradiction inherent in institution building, that "the institutions created in response to a crisis may not always directly relate to the problem area that generated the crisis" (Verba 1971, 306).

The relationship between the politics of institution building and the politics model presented here is so close as to suggest the presence of a unified model, but one to which the structural-functional approach brings a special relevance because of its original and longstanding concern for the processes of development and modernization in a cross-national context.

The structural-functional model, in the form described here, is directly parallel to the politics model in its attention to the nuts-and-bolts politics that underlies national development, decay, stasis, and change; although this would not be obvious if one treated structural-functionalism in terms of its own chosen vocabulary rather than the revised one used here. When such major works within a discipline arrive at similar solutions, even when they, for instance, start from the abstract early heights of traditional structural-functionalism, it suggests that collective theory development is not the impossibility it may seem to be.

Conclusion

Grand theories in political science have fallen from favor, and perhaps this is just as well, for they encouraged a kind of thinking that sought universality in concepts so abstract that they were empty. This chapter has shown, however, that grand theories are sometimes concrete as well, in the sense that everything theorists sought to explain at the macroanalytic level can be encompassed better by microanalytic models. A revisionist approach to structural-functional theory expands an appreciation of the capacity of the basic politics model, which can now be seen as adequate to the largest of research questions, such as political development, institutionalization, and democratic change. It also lays out in rather great detail some of the substance of the theory based on the politics model, and in so doing asks some interesting questions for future research.

Is there an empirical functionalism? What are the empirical 'needs' of different types of groups or systems? Would it be simpler to say that groups need direction and someone willing to give orders, rather than anything so olympian as 'rule execution' or 'rule adjudication'? Once there is a group leader, under what circumstances do functional 'opportunities' arise—for instance, to criticize the leader and rally around an opposing leader? What happens if functions are not met? Do all members of a group perceive the same functional needs? Can groups organize themselves without any formal government structure? If it is the role of a good theory to raise new questions, structural-functionalism may have done its work better than anyone noticed. Or perhaps any theory needs a little nudge from posterity to show forth its potential for generating research.

I have tried in this essay to show that a theory may contain more insights than it initially discloses. The work of the past by many fine students of comparative politics contained much that was useful despite its own conceptual apparatus, and it presented a potentially radical model of the political-developmental process. The axioms, definitions, and other propositions that have here been extricated from their original formulations need not be the end of a process but a beginning toward the creation of research-oriented comparative theory. This need impose no strictures and need result in no diminution of research freedom. But such a theory, handed from one comparative politics generation to the next, might serve as an example of the dynamic use of the past, to assist political research toward a more coherent future.

Notes

Another version of this chapter appeared in *Comparative Politics* 26, no. 4 (July 1994): 461–77. Reprinted by permission of Comparative Politics.

1. The Princeton Series in Political Development included, in the years prior to the Binder et al. (1971) volume, Pye (ed.) 1963, LaPalombara (ed.) 1963, Ward and Rustow (eds.) 1964, Coleman (ed.) 1965, Pye and Verba (eds.) 1965, and LaPalombara and Weiner (eds.) 1966.

2. The final two volumes were primarily composed of work by historians (Tilly 1974; Grew 1978).

3. David Easton, another of the systems-level theorists, has recently acknowledged that microanalytic approaches are in fact the correct social scientific approach; he argues only that the amount of detail is prohibitive, causing one to adopt systems theories as a second-best solution for their convenience in discussing whole societies (Easton 1990, 307, note 27).

4. Note how closely Weiner's formulation corresponds to the algorithmic model defined at the conclusion of Chapter 3.

5. LaPalombara's chapters are marked occasionally by his distancing himself from the structural-functional framework. He remarks, for example, "If we may be permitted the assumption that the three impulses we speak of (equality, capacity and differentiation) are empirically real and not merely a projection of the normative orientations of the authors of this volume, then . . ." (1971, 280).

6. Some rational-choice theorists believe that 'once the door is opened' any-

thing and everything may be defined as self-interest, and the rigor of the theory will be lost. Recent work has shown, however, that self-interest comes in but a handful of politically relevant forms (Lane 1992; Wildavsky 1987), so the use of the second structural-functional proposition becomes manageable in research terms and capable of precise foundation (see Chapter 4).

7. An exception is his attention to ideology and elite interaction, but the interelite conflict is not worked out in detail (1971, 238).

8. The concept of 'sequence' had largely disappeared from the structural-functional lexicon by the end of the Binder volume; the succeeding two volumes in the series put the nails firmly in its coffin (Tilly 1975; Grew 1978).

References

Almond, Gabriel A., and James S. Coleman, eds. 1960. *The Politics of the Developing Areas*. Princeton, NJ: Princeton University Press.

Almond, Gabriel A., and G. Bingham Powell Jr. 1966. *Comparative Politics: A Developmental Approach*. Boston: Little, Brown.

Baer, Michael A., Malcolm E. Jewell, and Lee Sigelman, eds. 1991. *Political Science in America: Oral Histories of a Discipline*. Lexington: University Press of Kentucky.

Bates, Robert H. 1981. *Markets and States in Tropical Africa: The Political Basis of Agricultural Policies*. Berkeley: University of California Press.

Bill, James A., and Robert L. Hardgrave Jr. 1973. *Comparative Politics: The Quest for Theory*. Columbus, OH: Charles E. Merrill.

Binder, Leonard, James, S. Coleman, Joseph LaPalombara, Lucien W. Pye, Sidney Verba, and Myron Weiner. 1971. *Crisis and Sequences in Political Development*. Princeton, NJ: Princeton University Press.

Coleman, James Smoot, ed. 1965. *Education and Political Development*. Princeton, NJ: Princeton University Press.

———. 1971. "The Development Syndrome: Differentiation-Equality-Capacity." In Binder et al. 1971, pp. 73–100.

Easton, David. 1990. *The Analysis of Political Structure*. New York: Routledge.

Finer, S. E. 1969–70. "Almond's Concept of 'The Political System': A Textual Critique." *Government and Opposition* 5 (Winter): 3–21.

Finifter, Ada W., ed. 1983. *Political Science: The State of the Discipline*. Washington, DC: American Political Science Association.

Flanagan, William, and Edwin Fogelman. 1967. "Functional Analysis." In *Contemporary Political Analysis*, ed. James C. Charlesworth, pp. 72–85. New York: The Free Press.

Foucault, Michel. 1973. *The Order of Things: An Archaeology of the Human Sciences*. New York: Vintage.

Grew, Raymond, ed. 1978. *Crises of Political Development in Europe and the United States*. Princeton, NJ: Princeton University Press.

Groth, Alexander J. 1970. "Structural Functionalism and Political Development: Three Problems." *Western Political Quarterly* 23 (September): 485–99.

Hempel, Carl G. 1959. "The Logic of Functional Analysis." In *Symposium in Sociological Theory*, ed. Llewellyn Gross, pp. 271–307. New York: Harper and Row.

Holt, Robert T., and John E. Turner. 1975. "Crises and Sequences in Collective Theory Development." *American Political Science Review* 69, no. 3 (September): 979–95.

Kahneman, Daniel, Paul Slovic, and Amos Tversky, eds. 1982. *Judgment Under Uncertainty: Heuristics and Biases.* Cambridge: Cambridge University Press.

Lane, Ruth. 1992. "Political Culture: Residual Category or General Theory?" *Comparative Political Studies* 25, no. 3 (October): 362–87.

———. 1994. "Structural-Functionalism Reconsidered: A Proposed Research Model." *Comparative Politics* 26, no. 4 (July): 461–77.

LaPalombara, Joseph, ed. 1963. *Bureaucracy and Political Development.* Princeton, NJ: Princeton University Press.

———. 1971. "Penetration: A Crisis of Governmental Capacity" and "Distribution: A Crisis of Resource Management." In Binder et al. 1971, pp. 205–82.

LaPalombara, Joseph, and Myron Weiner, eds. 1966. *Political Parties and Political Development.* Princeton, NJ: Princeton University Press.

Levi-Strauss, Claude. [1962] 1966. *The Savage Mind.* Chicago: University of Chicago Press.

Merton, Robert K. 1949. *Social Theory and Social Structure.* New York: The Free Press.

Migdal, Joel S. 1983. "Studying the Politics of Development and Change: The State of the Art." In Finifter 1983, pp. 309–38.

North, Douglass C., and Robert P. Thomas. 1973. *The Rise of the Western World: A New Economic History.* Cambridge: Cambridge University Press.

Parsons, Talcott. 1951. *The Social System.* Glencoe: Free Press.

Parsons, Talcott, and Edward Shils. 1951. *Toward a General Theory of Action.* Cambridge, MA: Harvard University Press.

Pye, Lucien W., ed. 1963. *Communications and Political Development.* Princeton, NJ: Princeton University Press.

———. 1971. "Identity and the Political Culture" and "The Legitimacy Crisis." In Binder et al. 1971, pp. 101–58.

Pye, Lucien W., and Sidney Verba, eds. 1965. *Political Culture and Political Development.* Princeton, NJ: Princeton University Press.

Tilly, Charles, ed. 1975. *Formation of National States in Western Europe.* Princeton, NJ: Princeton University Press.

Verba, Sidney. 1971. "Sequences and Development." In Binder et al. 1971, pp. 283–316.

Ward, Robert E., and Dankwart A. Rustow, eds. 1964. *Political Modernization in Japan and Turkey.* Princeton, NJ: Princeton University Press.

Weiner, Myron. 1971. "Political Participation: Crisis of the Political Process." In Binder et al. 1971, pp. 159–204.

Wildavsky, Aaron. 1987. "Choosing Preferences by Constructing Institutions: A Cultural Theory of Preference Formation." *American Political Science Review* 81, no. 1 (March): 3–21.

6 THE POLITICS MODEL AND A NEW PHILOSOPHY OF SCIENCE

In their relation to the philosophy of science, most political scientists resemble simple folks who live at the outskirts of a forest, a dark and very dangerous forest. Kings and barons and armies are known to live in the forest because people can hear the trumpets, the cannon fire, the clash of arms. Castles are sometimes glimpsed in fiery conflagration; walls are built and demolished; wise men and magicians are seen on battlements, consulting the stars and planets.

Anyone who ventures into the forest is apt to be in jeopardy, not because the combatants bear them any hostility, but because in the passion of battle, incautious travelers may be run down by an armor-plated warhorse and its knight, or be overwhelmed by a charge of halberdiers. As a result, when outsiders have business in the forest, they move with the greatest caution, speed, and dispatch.

In the period of ferment in political science that followed the Second World War and led to the behavioral revolution of the 1960s, political scientists determined that their endeavors needed the sanction of the highest authorities within science, those called the philosophers of science. Perhaps fearing that the forest was more dangerous than it actually was, political scientists made very brief trips into its depths and came back as quickly as possible with a set of rules to guide their research. The rules were helpful, but not immutable; the kings, barons, and wise men continued their discussions and often changed their minds. But political scientists, with a deference that would have impressed the forest's warriors had they noticed it, preferred to stick with the old rules rather than risk another foray into the dark byways of scientific philosophies.

Such behavior is understandable. If political scientists had wanted to be philosophers, they would have chosen that field in the first place. Not having so chosen, they feel they ought not to be required to traffic with various forms of philosophic discourse. But for those who have adhered to the rules called positivism, another visit to the forest will be necessary, because the rule givers have changed the rules. I try in this chapter to introduce this new dispensation, and perhaps to clarify slightly the nature of the battles fought.

Positivism and Science

In the debate over positivism within political science, a debate that began with the behavioral movement and continues today, political scientists have worked on the assumption that positivism was equivalent to 'science' and that any change in positivistic methods was a move away from the canons of science. This viewpoint entailed the conclusion that critics of behavioralism were arguing an antiscience position, trying to escape the rigors of positivism by urging various 'soft' alternatives that did not measure up as science. Both positivists and their critics have shared the view that they were arguing mainly over science, and not over positivism. As Ball remarks, either one was a behavioralist or one was left to associate with "Gadamer's hermeneutics, Habermas's Critical Theory . . . French deconstructionists, poststructuralists, and other similarly suspicious continental characters . . ." (Ball 1987, 2).[1]

Yet in the forty years since political scientists learned their first lessons in the philosophy of science, the philosophers have executed an about-face. They have officially declared logical positivism dead and buried. Musgrave speaks of its "demise" (1985, 197). Pitt says it has 'failed' (1988, 7). Kitcher believes it has "fallen on hard times" (1988, 167). Giere says there are today no voices to defend it (1988, 28). Suppe finds it irrelevant to actual science (1989, 45). Even Van Fraassen, a defender of empiricism, states that "logical positivism . . . even if one is quite charitable about what counts as a development rather than a change of position, has had a rather spectacular crash" (1980, 2). This goes beyond the developments with which political scientists are familiar (Feyerabend 1975; Kuhn 1962; Lakatos 1970; Laudan 1977) into an entirely new territory (Bloor 1976; Churchland 1979; Churchland and Hooker 1985; Giere 1988; Harre 1986; Hilton 1988; Pitt 1988; Suppe 1989; and the 'new' empiricist Van Fraassen 1980).

A greater familiarity with the terms of the arguments against positivism and in favor of scientific realism is useful in clarifying issues important to political science, such as the nature of theory, the role of data analysis, and the purposes to which scientific inquiry is directed. Behavioralism contained many separate strands, many of which were incompatible. A larger perspective on the positivist 'metaphysic,' in contrast to the new realist mode, explains and reconciles some of these differences. If positivism no longer exists except in occasional scientific backwaters, as Giere claims (1985, 97), political scientists may wish to consider whether their continued loyalty to positivism is appropriate, or whether there is room for alternative approaches to inquiry within political science.[2]

Disputes and New Directions

Students of political science have in recent years tended to be critical of both the direction and the achievements of the discipline (Blalock 1984; Gunnell 1986; Lindblom 1990; Lowi 1992; Ricci 1984). Much of this argument has in fact been over the positivistic methods brought in with the behavioral revolution, and much of it has been mooted by a new philosophy of science, which has replaced positivism in almost all scientific fields except political science.[3]

The approach that has in recent decades replaced positivism in the hearts and minds of philosophers of science is 'scientific realism,' and over recent years it has developed into a mature scientific metaphysic that contains much diversity but also is accorded general agreement among mainstream philosophers of science. This realism is of course not the ontological variety dating back to Plato, but an 'empirical' realism designed to explain the way modern science operates. It is important to emphasize that scientific realism is not a 'theory' that explains events in some specific field, but a full-fledged metaphysical position, a 'philosophy' of science. It does not answer questions about the causes or correlates of specific events but involves broader issues of 'what is meant by explanation?' (see Chapter 2).

As this transition from high positivism has taken place, much has changed in how science is understood. Gone is the emphasis on 'universal' laws (Giere 1988, 26–27; Kitcher 1988, 161–81; Railton 1988, 120). Gone is the hypothetico-deductive approach to explanation (Musgrave 1985, 221; Scriven 1988, 53–62). Gone is the positivists' emphasis on logical or linguistic theory statements (Churchland 1985, 45; Suppe 1989, 65–67). Gone is the rigid emphasis on falsifiability

(Hooker 1985, 156; Pitt 1988, 3–4). Gone is the contention that theoretical statements are separate from observation statements (Churchland 1979, 127–28; Hooker 1985, 157). Gone is the neutrality of the scientist (see Giere 1988, 22–28; Pitt 1988; Suppe 1989, 38–77).

In their place scientific realism emphasizes model-theoretic forms of explanation, the search for causal processes that underlie and explain observed phenomena, and the creative role of the scientific community not as a source of political subjectivity but as a moral force in the progressive search for knowledge about the real world (Bhaskar 1975; Churchland 1979; Giere 1988, 62–91; Harre 1986). Many of these ideas will be separately familiar to political scientists, but the degree to which the ideas form a coherent approach to science is less well known. No longer is it necessary for social scientists to argue the negative position against positivism or behavioralism, the 'let us do something different, anything but positivism' argument. A well-developed alternative is available in scientific realism.

The upshot of the change from positivism to realism among the philosophers of science is that it has now become possible to qualify as a scientist without being a positivist. And this conclusion is drawn from the philosophers' study of physics, astronomy, chemistry, and the other physical sciences; from the hardest of the 'hard' sciences. These developments in the philosophy of science do not at all mean that positivism was 'wrong,' or indeed that realism is 'right,' but they do place positivism in a new context, one that makes it a single stage in an ongoing inquiry rather than an absolute solution to questions of scientific method. This growth and continuity is emphasized by the fact that Hempel and Popper, the canonical fathers of positivism, can both be understood as the originators of scientific realism on the basis of their original and subsequent writings (Churchland 1979, x; Kitcher 1988, 167; Suppe 1989, 338).[4]

Does the Change Matter?

How might these changes in modern metaphysics affect political science? Several possibilities exist. Scientific realism sanctions a procedure already adopted 'without authorization' by many political scientists, the procedure of 'full speed ahead and damn the philosophers'—in other words, the idea that working scientists themselves should define their field and methods because they know more about them than do the philosophers. Equally important, scientific realism enlarges the scope of science: It does not make science any 'easier' or less rigorous, but it expands and deepens the range of approaches that are defined as scientific. Scientific realism takes particular aim at the positivist reduction of 'theory' to the documentation of observable correlations between variables, a practice that has often troubled political scientists who were otherwise predisposed positively toward scientific goals. Scientific realism also is relevant to political science because realism devotes much greater attention to theory than did positivism, and theory is intended to describe complex real-world processes, not just define correlational regularities.

These changes of direction, or at least of emphasis, tend to put the contemporary conduct of political science in a new light. Practices that were thought to be unquestionably scientific, such as massive data collections and highly sophisticated statistical methods of analysis, are less central to scientific realism than they were for positivistic behavioralism; practices that were thought to be dubiously scientific, such as the emphasis on the meaning of political actions to the subjects themselves, are given greater legitimacy. Gunnell (1986, 15–16, 50) has commented on the unfamiliarity of most political scientists with the rough-and-ready practices of physical scientists, and the tendency of political scientists to be unduly subservient to rationalistic philosophers (see also Pye 1968, 240–41). For these very reasons, scientific realism raises for political science new options, new alternatives, and a better understanding of what actually happens in the everyday practice of the older sciences.

Caution needs to be employed in evaluating the realist literature because there are many varieties (metaphysical, internal, constructive, semantic, modal, and so on), and the waters are muddied by some purely ideological attempts to use realism not as a scientific method but as a theory that leads to certain conclusions. Wendt and Shapiro (1993, 1) have, for instance, warned against the claims by neo-Marxists and structuration theorists "that realism either entails their social theories or predisposes us to accept their truth." Because of these easy invitations to misinterpret scientific realism, for a brief space it is necessary to closet ourselves with the official philosophers of science and see why they grew disillusioned with positivism, and how scientific realism emerged.

Preliminary Definitions

To start the discussion off, it is helpful to look at some informal definitions of realism. Hooker graphically sums up the central difference
between scientific realists and the logical or empirical positivists:
"[R]ealists hold that the surface merely dazzles and should not beguile
anyone into mistaking it for reality. Empiricists, contrariwise, hold that
the depths are ghostly, having no independent rationale for their vener-
ation beyond the surface through which they indirectly appear"
(Hooker 1985, 153). Other definitions extend this theme: Realists want
"to describe things as they really are," "to see bare reality" with the
veil of appearance stripped away (Ellis 1985, 48). Harre, a major expo-
nent of the scientific realist view, emphasizes the scientific search for
"real causal mechanisms," the internal constitution of things, rather
than the positivist correlations between observable data. "For prediction we need to know only facts of the same kind as those we wish to
predict, . . . observable symptoms. But to explain we need to know the
causal mechanism that produces the symptoms . . ." (1988, 139). Positivism, Harre argues, would have stopped malaria research with the
correlation between swamps and fever, never discovering the plasmo-
dium and the mosquito carrying it (1988, 131).

Van Fraassen, despite or perhaps because of his position as a well-
known critic of scientific realism, gives a careful definition of its central belief "that theories account for the phenomena (which means the
observable processes and structures) by postulating other processes
and structures not directly accessible to observation; and that a system
of any sort is described by a theory in terms of its possible states"
(1980, 3). In the extreme form of scientific realism, Van Fraassen
continues, "science aims to give us, in its theories, a literally true story
of what the world is like; and acceptance of a scientific theory involves
the belief that it is true" (1980, 8).[5]

In his now-classic exposition, Roy Bhaskar (1975) stated such early
and extreme principles of realist ontology as "that perception gives us
access to things and experimental activity access to structures that exist
independently of us" (1975, 9). Science is "a process in motion, continually on the move from manifest behavior to essential nature, from
the description of things . . . to . . . possible explanations and thus the
discovery of the mechanisms responsible for them" (1975, 248). The
claim to be in touch with the 'real' world was difficult to maintain and

has now been abandoned, but the implications for research were straightforward: Scientific realists saw reality as stratified, and their purpose was to probe deeper and deeper into the underlying nature of things.

Bhaskar illustrates this from the field of chemistry, where the first explanation level for the reaction between sodium and hydrochloric acid is simply descriptive: "$2Na + 2HCl = 2NaCl + H_2$." A deeper level of explanation is the theory of atomic number and valency; a next deeper is the theory of electrons; and a still deeper explanatory level is subatomic theories (1975, 169).

Scientific Differences

Philosophies of science are not, however, bricks that exist in absolute isolation from one another. Rather, positivism and scientific realism are composed of webs of ideas made up of various individual strands, some structural, some secondary. The movement from one philosophy of science to another therefore proceeds not in a single step, but in an incremental reevaluation of individual tenets. These specific issues include (1) the possibility and desirability of 'universal' laws; (2) the nature, sources, uses, and meaning of theory; (3) the logical-linguistic or model-theoretic form in which theory is expressed; (4) the distinction between theoretical and observational languages and the assumption that observation is neutral, unaffected by theoretic concepts; (5) the related observable-nonobservable distinction in respect to scientific entities; (6) whether the goal of science is prediction or explanation; (7) how scientific findings are to be justified; and (8) whether the philosophy of science is a normative objective discipline or a descriptive scientific discipline.

Scientists schooled in the classics of positivism have an acquired resistance to the idea of a philosophy of science that changes over time because positivists presented themselves, inadvertently or not, as advocates of a universal method, one that was not transient but more or less absolute. Yet scientific metaphysics has a long and varied history, from the disagreement between Aristotle and Eudoxus on the best way to explain astronomical data (Suppe 1989, 20–21) to the troubled period in early modern science when the 'old science' was shaken by the triumph of Copernican over Ptolemaic astronomy. Students of this period suggest that this overthrow of accepted ideas—if Ptolemy is wrong, who may not be wrong?—led philosophers to an especially acute concern not so much with knowledge itself as with the ways of justifying knowledge, of certifying it as absolute (Giere 1988, 23; Suppe 1989, 392).

The logical positivists' answer to the demand for justified knowledge has developed over decades under various titles that maintained a set of common core beliefs about the proper conduct of science. Called initially the Popper–Hempel or the hypothetico-deductive (HD) method, or logical positivism or logical empiricism, the method is now often referred to, perhaps with a trace of mockery, as the Received View (e.g. Suppe 1989, 38–62) or the Official View (e.g., Kitcher 1988, 167). Despite differences of emphasis and modifications over succeeding years, the core of this approach remained the covering law model (Hempel 1965, 135–75 and 412–25; Hempel and Oppenhein 1988).

It is chastening to see within how brief a time all the major pillars of positivism fell. One major set of issues involved rejection of the possibility of 'neutral' observation statements, and thereby the possibility of clear falsification of theoretic statements. A second problem area involved the growing conviction that 'real' science had in fact never proceeded as the positivists said it did, with deductive methods, rigorous logic, and in accord with universal principles of method. Hooker has summarized the major criticisms against classical logical positivism; as may be seen, the indictment is far-reaching.

> The chief objections to the positivist theory of science are: (1) theories are not definitionally reducible to finitely, observationally verifiable assertions; (2) scientific method is not rationally confinable to entailment from the facts; (3) observation is not a fundamental, transparent category but a complex, anthropomorphic process, itself investigated by science; (4) historical intertheory relations do not fit the accumulative model; (5) accepted observationally based facts do not belong to an eternal, theory-free category but are theory laden and subject to theoretical criticism. To these I would especially add the criticism (6, 7) that science is not isolated from the human individual and from society in the manner presupposed by positivism; (8) that method is not rationally universal either across science at a time or across history; (9) that logic does not have the privileged status given it by positivism but is itself open to broadly empirical investigation; and (10) that there is not the gulf between the normative and the descriptive presupposed by positivism. (Hooker 1985, 156–57)

I will return to these issues in making comparisons between logical positivism and scientific realism on some of the major issues involved. First, however, it is appropriate to review the manner in which the changes developed.

Changes in Scientific Attitudes

Thomas Kuhn's book on the structure of scientific revolutions (1962) was of course the defining first event in the challenge to logical positivism, and it was followed by clashes between Kuhn and a series of philosophers of science who worked to make logical positivism acceptable in light of Kuhn's criticism. The general line of this debate is familiar to political scientists in Lakatos's (1970) research program, and Laudan's (1977) research tradition. The issues underlying this debate are helpfully analyzed by Giere (1988) in terms of two dimensions: (1) *the nature of theory,* whether it really represents the world ('realism') or is just a convenience in summarizing known facts ('instrumentalism'); and (2) *the nature of science,* whether it is rational and objective ('rationalism') or only the subjective consensus of the community ('naturalism'). Use of these two dimensions clarifies who was revolutionary, and just what they might have been revolutionary (or conservative) about. Kuhn, for instance, was not wholly radical: He attacked the rationality of science but maintained the instrumentalist view of theory characteristic of positivism, that theories were mere instruments of research not tied directly to real phenomena. Lakatos, in turn, tried to reassert the rationality of science, in making the research 'program' a doctrine of rational progress, reacting against the forces of irrationality. Laudan's research 'tradition' shifts the balance toward a sociology of science where community consensus is decisive, but he never goes so far as to deny the basic rationality of science (Giere 1988, 40–41).

An important factor in the current changes in the philosophy of science has been the sociology, or psychology, of science, and the associated general interest in the actual history of science, although there has been considerable discontinuity within these subdisciplines. The sociology of knowledge associated with the name of Mannheim (1936) had Marxian origins and was not directly connected with the sociological approach to scientific behavior found in the work of Robert Merton (1957). The field's lack of popularity may have been associated with the positivist hegemony, which discounted subjective factors in the development of scientific knowledge.

The original positivist approach, going back to Frege, made a sharp distinction between logic and psychology, and it intended that each be studied separately. But though the logical aspect of scientific practice was highly developed in logical positivism, the psychology of science did not develop at all (Giere 1988, 23–30) until the impact of the Kuhnian revolution restored attention to the subjective aspects of science and a number of writers took up the detailed study of actual historical practices and attitudes.

The Edinburgh "strong program" in the sociology of knowledge directly challenged the distinction between logic and sociology, arguing that scientists' beliefs were determined by their interests, both class interests and professional interests. The school was so radical that even mathematics was reinterpreted in line with the naturalistic approach (Bloor 1976, 74–94; see also Giere 1988, 50–57). Similarly, the statistical controversy between Pearson and Yule over the treatment of nominal data was attributed not to conceptual issues but to their conflicting attitudes toward eugenics and its relation to the social status of professional and traditional elite groups (see the discussion in Shapin 1982, 190). The so-called "Paris school" modifies the strong program to take into account the effects of scientific knowledge upon the social microstructure (Harre 1986, 9–13). Other historians of science describe the sociological struggle within a scientific community as a Darwinian battle based partly "on a desire to understand the world in which we live," but also involving the desire to 'get credit' for one's own contributions and the desire to see that no competitor gets any credit to which he or she is not entitled (Hull 1988, 305).

Some Comparisons

The issues that separate positivism from scientific realism are now well thrashed out in the philosophic literature. The major issues have included the meaning of 'truth' (Churchland 1985, 35; Ellis 1985, 53; Harre 1996, 6; Hooker 1985, 191); the nature of explanation (Giere 1985, 95; Musgrave 1985, 221; Scriven 1988, 53–62); the form of theory (Churchland 1985, 45; Suppe 1989, 65–67); the use of universal laws (Kitcher 1988, 168, 181); the appropriateness of falsifiability and justification (Hooker 1985, 156; Pitt 1988, 3–4); the role of theory in observation and the use of nonobservable variables (Glymour 1985, 100; Hacking 1985; Suppe 1989, 62); and the nature of induction

(Giere 1988, 264; Suppe 1989, 391–93). These separate strands can be woven together somewhat to shorten the length of the discussion.

One of the earliest challenges to the hypothetico-deductive method was Churchland's (1979) influential work in which he attacked a basic pillar of the positivist creed, the belief that the theoretical and observational languages were epistemologically different from one another. In the Received View, observational terms and statements were seen as uninfected by theory or subjectivity; they provided an objective grounding by which theoretical statements, seen as artificial and 'instrumental,' could be connected to reality by correspondence rules, and thus tested (Giere 1988, 25–26; Suppe 1989, 62). Of all the positivists' beliefs this theoretical-observational distinction was among the most basic because it created the possibility of theory falsification and thereby the progress of science through the rejection of untrue theories. Churchland's attack on this tenet was total: Perceptions are themselves theoretical, he argued. "[T]he adequacy of our perceptual judgments is in part a matter of the adequacy of the background theory (conceptual framework) in whose terms they happen to be framed." Observation statements no longer have any "privileged status as independent and theory-neutral arbiters of what there is in the world" (1979, 2). In addition Churchland attacked the idea, also fundamental to positivism, that theory could or should be stated in linguistic, sentential, or logical forms. Drawing on child development psychology to emphasize the range of intellectual activity that takes place prior to language acquisition, Churchland used the "plasticity of mind" of the title to undercut orthodox empiricism by arguing that there are "an infinite number of mutually incommensurable observation vocabularies," each with a different set of assumptions and none more objective than any other (1979, 140).

The grandest issue on which the two schools differed was the nature, form, and purpose of theory itself. The positivists, of course, worked in terms of universal statements from which deductions could be made about specific phenomena, but this position struck most of the realists as impossible partly because of the difficulty of finding laws that were timeless and unconditioned, partly because real science did not appear in fact to develop in this manner. The realists strongly resisted the positivists' definition of theory as an artificial, man-made entity, and they saw theory as a natural reflection of what was 'really' going on in the real world.

Words or Models

A major shift in this respect was the scientific realists' insistence that the linguistic form of positivist theory was a limitation that should be transformed by a shift to the idea of theoretic 'models,' made if necessary of "bits of wire, metal, and cardboard," as in the case of the double helix model (Giere 1985, 91). While models may for convenience be expressed in linguistic form, realists define them in terms of abstract concepts that map real dynamic processes. This view has been sufficiently convincing that modern empiricists largely accept it, although disagreeing on technical points (Suppe 1989, 348; Van Fraassen 1980, 41–69).

There is a fundamental difference between positivists and realists, however, in the type of entities that are appropriate to model and theory construction, and the difference points to a difficulty with the observable-nonobservable distinction. Where empiricists are committed to the idea that only observable phenomena need be studied, realists are committed to a more fundamental reality beneath perceived phenomena, to ever deeper structural levels of explanation.

Originally, of course, it was just such 'metaphysical' entities against which the strictures of logical positivism were directed; but over the years the discoveries in physics and chemistry and other natural sciences made it very difficult to deny the scientific status of unobservable phenomena. And it is often difficult to determine just what is meant by 'observable.' Atoms are not directly observable, so must they be denied? Strict adherence to the observability doctrine leads to the idea that "the back of the moon did not exist before the Apollo fly-pasts, nor did bacteria [exist] before the invention of the microscope" (Harre 1986, 57; see also Hacking 1985, 132–52). The advocates for using nonobservable entities have thus largely won this particular battle.[6]

Whether theory is simply a research convenience for summarizing data or is designed to capture the operations of the real world remains a lively issue, although no longer a truly metaphysical one. Van Fraassen, who continues to vigorously argue an empiricist position (though no longer the classical positivist variant), bases his objection to the realist definition of theory on the idea that it encourages unlimited demands for explanatory depths and for explanations "which would produce the metaphysical baggage of hidden parameters that carry no new empirical import" (1980, 23, 31).

It is notable here how the whole semantics of theory has shifted from the positivists' emphasis on theories as things that exist only to be falsified, until one survives and can be justified as true; and the realists' emphasis on theory as a coherent explanatory structure that fits like a glove over reality, without any serious consideration of whether it is 'true' so long as it works reasonably well to explain whatever events are in question. Emphasis has also shifted away from the process of induction by which new universal statements were developed to a belief that theories are made up not of isolated universal laws but integrated wholes composed of a mixture of theoretic and empirical elements.

The New Emphasis on Explanation

All these themes are brought together under the general heading of 'explanation,' which is of central importance to scientific realists. The logical positivists were of course interested in explanation. Explanation was exactly what the whole covering law model was said to produce. But in the distinction made earlier, logical positivists often seemed more interested in justifying their explanations than in having them, and this was one of the features of logical positivism that so offended working physical scientists. Popper, especially, presents a view of theories piled about in ample heaps, with the scientist's only task to sift the good from the bad; in fact, most scientists feel, theories are scarce and hard to come by (Giere 1985, 87). Lakatos went some way toward strengthening theoretical research against the falsificationist obsession, but the scientific realists wanted to go much further.

In this inquiry the realists were hampered by the inherent ambiguity of the idea of explanation. In the old rationalist model an explanation was absolute; in the naturalistic model, however, explanation was inescapably social, with the acceptability of the explanation depending on the persons to whom one was explaining, what their interests were, how much they knew already, and so on. The basis of explanation is, for realists, description of the phenomenal world. This, of course, is its basic difference with hard-core empiricism, which seeks only data summaries and predictability. Explanation should be more than description, Scriven argues, but explanation "sometimes consists simply in giving the *right* description," which is "the one which fills in a particular gap in the understanding of the person or people to whom the explanation is directed" and which makes clear "something not previously clear." The crucial idea is that of "understanding," which Scriven admits is difficult to identify precisely. Yet understanding "is *not* a subjectively appraised state any more than knowing is; both are objectively testable and are, in fact, tested in examinations" (Scriven 1988, 53). Though some academics downplay the importance of examinations, the point is nonetheless a telling one: Understanding is not a mystical concept—we know it, and we use it regularly.[7]

More Not Less Science

Realists frequently emphasize that explanation requires *more* than prediction—that realism, though it is antipositivist, is not antiscientific but *more vigorously scientific* than positivism. Theoretic explanation ought to provide "some insight into the structure and workings of the mechanism, above and beyond the capability of predicting and controlling its outcomes" (Railton 1988, 120). To say one wants an 'account' of a mechanism is not necessarily vague; it involves increasing the details of the description of the causal claim to characterize the process more fully (Railton 1988, 120).

That the scientific realist approach to explanation is not simply a replay of the positivist-subjectivist controversy results from the realists' appreciation of the (legitimate) role of the scientific community in evaluating alternative explanations. In respect to this scientific community, which effectively decides what counts as a good explanation, Harre takes the highest ground, arguing that science is "a distinctive moral order, whose main characteristic is the trust that obtains among its members." Science, he argues, "has a special status, not because it is a sure way of producing truths and avoiding falsehood, but because it is a communal practice of a community with a remarkable and rigid morality ... a commitment that the products of this community shall be trustworthy" (1986, 6).

The focus on the scientific community has opened the issue of the cognitive behavior of scientists, primarily to inquire whether scientists think in the same ways as laypersons, or differently. Churchland insists scientists think 'better' than laypeople and gives a rather extended example of how ordinary folks can learn to see with scientific eyes; for instance tilting the visual plane when watching sunsets, in order to school themselves to see, correctly, that the earth moves and not the sun (Churchland 1979, 30–34). Others believe scientists are more similar to laypeople than they may think (Turnbull and Slugowski 1988, 66–68); Giere develops a cognitive approach that studies scientific decision making as "an exercise of ordinary human judgment" (1988, xvii).

Scientific Realism and Political Science

When traditional political science set out, some decades ago, on the behavioralist journey to transform the study of politics, it proceeded hand-in-hand with the philosophy of science. The choice of such companionship demonstrated a commendable determination to proceed according to the highest scientific canons, but it may have put the cart before the horse. By adopting a scientific metaphysic, logical positivism, which was directed almost exclusively at the most advanced of the physical sciences, political science denied itself the liberty (which the physical sciences had enjoyed) of developing according to its own internal dynamics.

Yet the impact of positivism was initially progressive. In those sciences that still emphasized traditional approaches, positivism served to shake up the establishment sufficiently that room was made for new ideas and approaches, as illustrated in a recent collection of oral histories by a number of elder political scientists who were 'present at the creation' of behavioralism (Baer, Jewel, and Sigelman 1991).

Positivism and behavioralism stimulated political research, sending scientists out to study the American electorate, where their discoveries revised the discipline's understanding of the nature of democracy (Campbell, Converse, Miller, and Stokes 1964; Stouffer 1963), and encouraging theoretical innovations (Downs 1957; Riker 1962); yet there was a negative side. By the 1980s critics had begun to suggest that behavioralism, defined in positivist terms, had tended to cripple the creativity of political research (Ball 1987; Gunnell 1986; Hardin 1987; Lindblom and Cohen 1979; Pye 1990). Indeed, the problems of applying positivist precepts in the social sciences have been one direct source of the challenge to positivism.

Philosophers of science are overwhelmingly from the physical sciences and mathematics, and the hold of positivism could not really be broken until the 'hard' scientists decided the time had come to replace it; only they had the scientific legitimacy to tell the philosophers, 'No, you are wrong, science does not work as you have tried to tell us it does.' But social scientists, too, have participated in the critique of positivism both by direct and indirect attack. Among the direct attacks have been those that assailed various of positivism's precepts, such as universal laws and falsificationism, or the one-sided emphasis on variable correlation (Brown 1979; D'Andrade 1986, 19–29; Donagan 1964; Jessor 1991, 3–18; Nelson 1975; Root 1993, 107–11; Secord 1986, 199–200; Winch 1958).

The indirect attacks, less noticed, have taken the form of proposing alternative methods for the pursuit of knowledge about social phenomena (Eckstein 1975; Eulau 1986; Farr 1987; Moon 1975; Sylvan and Glassner 1985). What has weakened many of these attacks has been the belief, held both by critics and defenders of positivism, that a move away from positivism was a move away from science. Positivism has had the benefit, therefore, of support by persons who did not fully agree with its approach but believed that serious criticism would be equivalent to rejecting 'science' (exceptions include Isaac 1987 and Sayer 1992). The development of scientific realism as an alternative model of science allows this discussion to be placed in a new light. It also makes plain that some social scientists who adopted positivistic language but wanted "to modify it a little" were not engaged in modification only, but in a shift to a new metaphysic.

The reader who is not fond of dancing with philosophers on the head of their pin must wonder if metaphysics matters. Cannot the discipline simply go its way without attending to the somewhat esoteric concerns of the philosophers? This is a weighty argument, because scientific realism itself has been the result of a revolt by scientists, deep in their research, against philosophers' trying to run their research lives. Yet at least some attention to philosophical issues can be helpful (1) in saving a discipline from unproductive quarrels, particularly among those who believe they have a corner on true scientific method; (2) in opening up a new appreciation for the larger world of theory and explanation; and (3) in providing guidance to those who seek it, in respect to the goals of different theories and methods, and in encouraging them to a reasonable consistency with their assumptions.[8]

New Direction and Possibilities

Political science's discontent with itself is now of sufficiently long duration to be of some educational value. Behavioralism once appeared to be 'the solution' to this discontent, but today even hard-core behavioralists are looking for additions, if not alternatives, to their methodological pursuits. What is wanted seems to be something that is scientific without being unrealistically narrow, something that maintains intellectual rigor without leaching away from the political process everything that makes it interesting. Political scientists have looked everywhere in their search—have looked to economics, to anthropology, to statistics, to mathematics. The only place they have not investigated thoroughly is their own back yard, where the 'politics model' has been quietly available as an alternative method, if anyone should choose to notice it.

The greater openness of the scientific realist philosophy of science directs a spotlight on this unnoticed corner of the political science discipline. Where the politics model was largely outlawed by positivism's insistence on universal laws, axiomatic theory structures, and vigorous falsificationism, the politics model takes on a central importance under the alternative scientific roof of realism. And, as the foregoing discussion has made plain, realists see their position as *more rather than less rigorous* than positivism, so that the politics model must be understood as scientifically progressive, providing stricter research guidelines, and ensuring adherence to the scientific realist axiom of explanation in depth. Scientific realism is not a 'refuge' from rigor but a further step in understanding the rigors of scientific practice. Where positivism judged research on statistical significance, which could be satisfied by correlations between variables that were conveniently available, realism demands scientific significance, a deeper search into actual political processes, and the development of explanations that satisfy an audience of peers, laypersons, and officials, all of whom demand real answers.

The emphasis on political processes will be the major practical guide for research, under the politics model. The positivistic imperative that so creatively took political scientists out into the electorate to discover 'the American voter' will be supplemented (but not replaced) by attention to real citizens and real politicians in their actual political circumstances. Rather than background demographic variables and political attitudes, political scientific realists will bring back into view the actual interactions by which political societies are created, maintained, and destroyed. The emphasis on institutions is a natural part of this inquiry, where institutions are understood as human processes and not as idealized or hypostatized entities with some 'higher' rationality of their own. For the scientific realists, institutions are a mechanism, a process, within which and upon which individual actors pursue their goals.

The insistence that political scientists attend to the epistemological commitments under which they work is not simple nitpicking; it involves the researcher's consciousness of exactly what he or she is doing, and the rights and responsibilities attendant thereon.

What Next for the Politics Model?

The opportunities suggested by the politics model may be grouped at three levels of analysis. At a first level, the politics model may be amplified by replication of its basic approach in new subject areas—additional areas of the world for comparativists, additional institutions for Americanists, additional agencies and programs for students of public administration, and additional intergovernmental institutions for students of international politics. Such analyses will continue a long tradition within political science of increasing the descriptive range of its studies but will discipline such studies, with a light hand, by directing attention toward explication of the concrete logic of political interaction, and by encouraging the search for general patterns of behavior. As Eckstein neatly says, in a related context, "more thought, more imagination, more logic, less busy-work" (1975, 123).

At a second level, the politics model calls for more 'depth excavation' into the infrastructure of political interaction. If the model entertains wider ranges of motivations, for instance, inquiry must pursue the exact nature of these motivations, and their measurement (see, for example, Wildavsky 1987). If informal rules and informal institutions are important, inquiry needs to delve into the exact nature of such rule sets; inquiry must not be content merely to affirm the importance of rules and institutions, but willing to capture them in operational, empirical terms.

At a final level of analysis the politics model encourages the development of structural hypotheses that summarize and abstract the results of descriptive analyses so that truly cross-situational conclusions may be drawn. The international relations theorists, with their long interest in the systemic characteristics of political aggregates, will be major resources here. Such summary work, based on concrete political phenomena but conscious also of the patterns into which those phenomena fall, may stand as a partial answer to Easton's recent call for structural models, allowing political science to rise above its data rather than drown in it (Easton 1990, 257–58).

Notes

Another version of this chapter appeared in the *Journal of Theoretical Politics* 8, no. 3 (July 1996). Reprinted by permission of Sage Publications.

1. The language here is not intended to obscure the difference between positivism and behavioralism, because of course the two are not the same—positivism is a metaphysical position and behavioralism a methodological school. For simplicity of discourse, and because their connection was so close in political science, however, the terms are sometimes used interchangeably here. Nor do I intend to suggest that positivism was a unified approach (see the discussion below). By way of perspective, it is interesting to recall that argument over method has been going on since 1880 at the least (Somit and Tanenhaus 1967, 29–31).

2. The new approach of scientific realism does not diminish the value of recent methodology texts (e.g., King, Keohane, and Verba 1994) that seek to improve empirical methods in qualitative research in political science.

3. Some political scientists, such as Eulau (1986), thought that positivism was and still is the answer to the discipline's problems; but Eulau, for instance, is one of the few political scientists with the independence to take the positivist canon lightly and to give his own research concerns primacy. His emphasis on the political "process" suggests that his independence has led him very close to scientific realist theory as defined here.

4. The new student of scientific realism is apt to be disconcerted by the discovery that the same Hempel who crafted logical positivism is also considered a founder of realism, and that Popper makes a claim to having always been a realist. The apparent inconsistency is readily explained by studying again some of the original texts, where a very wide variety of ideas, suggestions, and questions about the nature of science are closely mixed. Where initially Hempel was read with attention on the "summary" paragraphs, which formalized the covering law, the emphasis is now, from the scientific realist point of view, on the deeper issues of explanation that stood elbow to elbow with the covering law in Hempel's text. Hempel's work can be seen today, with the benefit of hindsight, as raising many of the issues now featured by scientific realists, for instance, in defining explanation as "one of the foremost objectives of empirical science," answering "the question 'why?' rather than only the question 'what?' " (Hempel and Oppenhein 1988, 9). The examples of explanation provided by Hempel are of the same sort raised now by scientific realists; compare Hempel's explanations of why, when a mercury thermometer is dropped in hot water, the mercury briefly falls before rising rapidly, or why an oar appears bent in water, with Friedman's (1988) 'Why does water boil?' or Scriven's (1988) inquiry into why bridges collapse. In gen-

eral, indeed, Hempel's actual text is much less rigid than the hypothetico-deductive model it helped to create. This is shown in Hempel's well-known essay "Theoretician's Dilemma," where he flatly rejects the positivist's argument that intervening (theoretical) variables should be discarded and the empirical correlations alone retained (Hempel 1965, 173–226). On Hempel's 'realistic' leanings see also Kitcher (1988, 167) and Suppe (1989, 21).

The case of Karl Popper is similarly ambiguous in respect to positivism, for while he gave great prominence to the requirement of falsifiability, which was so central to the positivist program, Popper has always been a realist in the direct sense of one who believes in the real world and in objective truth (Popper 1972). A recent study by a friend and colleague of Popper's argues that Popper's interest in falsification was somewhat transient, directed toward refuting theories he opposed, such as "various Platonists, Hegelians, Marxists, sociologists of knowledge, and wholesale planners" (Simkin 1993, 3), and that his real interest was in the trial-and-error growth of scientific knowledge, based on scientific models quite comparable to those now advocated by scientific realists (Popper 1972, 64–69). What made Popper seem positivist was his absolute agreement with Hume on the question of induction; this meant theories emerged virtually from nowhere, or, as one student suggests, were comparable to 'Darwinian' genetic mutations (Miller 1983, 15).

5. This 'metaphysical' realism, with its emphasis on 'truth,' was easy to attack and hard to defend and has been replaced with versions that view the truth of a theory as a goal rather than as a fact (Ellis 1985, 51–53; Giere 1988, 77–78).

6. Empiricists conversely mock the realists as similar to Thomas Aquinas, trying to prove the existence of God (Van Fraassen 1980, 204–15).

7. The current status of the debate between realism and empiricism on the issue of explanation can be seen in a comparison of the approach taken by Frederick Suppe, an avowed if reconstructed realist, and the approach of Bas Van Fraassen, an avowed and equally reconstructed antirealist. Suppe's "constructive realism," which he also calls the "semantic conception," developed as an alternative to logical positivism and takes particular exception to the positivists' definition of theories as linguistic entities. 'Semantic' is used by Suppe in the sense of 'formal,' and "the heart of a theory is an extralinguistic theory structure" that specifies "the admissible behaviors of state transition systems." For example, in particle physics a system is characterized as 'n' bodies with three position and momentum coordinate variables that specify the state of the system and specify change patterns (Suppe 1989, 4). For Suppe the goal of realist explanation is "counterfactuality": One wants to explain "how the phenomena would have behaved had the idealized conditions been met" so that one can explain system behavior over time (65–66). One is concerned not with "the velocity with which the milk bottle actually fell" but with "the velocity with which it would have fallen had it fallen in a vacuum, had it been a point-mass, and so on" (68–69).

Bas Van Fraassen's "constructive empiricism" represents a wide variety of changes in the Received View of positivism yet maintains that view's central focus on first-order-observable phenomena. The logical positivists "were right to think in some cases that various philosophical perplexities, misconceived as problems in ontology and epistemology, were really at bottom problems about language," but they went too far in thinking all philosophical problems could be turned into language problems (1980, 3). For Van Fraassen the criterion for accepting a scientific theory is that the theory "saves the phenomena," that is, it brings together the observable data into a coherent whole (4). The search for causes should not be "a demand for explanation which would produce the metaphysical baggage of hidden parameters that carry no new empirical import" (31). This directly rejects the realists' belief in deeper realities.

When it comes to evaluating theories, Van Fraassen introduces the notion of "empirical adequacy," but he accepts the shift to model-theoretic explanation as do the realists (see the discussion of Van Fraassen in Churchland 1985, 45).

> To present a theory is to specify a family of structures, its models; and secondly, to specify certain parts of those models (the empirical substructures) as candidates for the direct representation of observable phenomena. The structure which can be described in experimental and measurement reports we can call appearances: the theory is empirically adequate if it has some model such that all appearances are isomorphic to empirical substructures of that model. (Van Fraassen 1980, 64)

"Science gives us a picture of the world as a net of interconnected events, related to each other in a complex but orderly way" (123). Finally he suggests that "an explanation often consists in listing salient factors, which point to a *complete story* of how the event happened," and this eliminates various hypotheses (129). The diligent reader will perhaps at this point wonder whether much difference is left between realists and empiricists. The differences, while philosophically urgent to the protagonists, do not necessarily have heavy significance for the actual conduct of research. The grand issue of how 'real' is the real world separates the two schools, but it is expressed primarily in terms of how vigorously explanation can be pursued; and the empiricists are generally seen as trying to avoid the lessons of simple common sense by trying to deny causal explanation (Musgrave 1985, 221). The major difference for practical research is the number of 'aspects' of the real world that the explanation must reach; constructive realism says the model must reach 'many or most' aspects; constructive empiricism requires only that observable aspects be included (Giere 1985, 80–82).

8. A case in point is Jon Elster, well known for his work in rational-choice theory. Yet a recent work (1989) suggests that he has so modified rational-choice theory that his approach no longer fits in the same classification and is better categorized as a case of scientific realism. Why is this so? Elster's book opens with a chapter on mechanisms, the 'nuts and bolts' of his title, and the major theme of the whole book is "explanation by mechanisms." Social science, he says, "like other empirical sciences," deals in two kinds of phenomena: "events" such as the election of George Bush, and "states of affairs" such as the majority of Republicans in the electorate (the examples are Elster's). One approach to explanation would be to explain Bush's election by the Republican majority. This correlational approach, which Elster does not label as positivistic although it clearly fits under that rubric, is laid aside. Instead, he says, there is a more fundamental approach, explaining the Republican majority "as being the result of a series of events, each of which took the form of belief formation by an individual voter." This latter approach "is logically prior to explaining facts" and explains an event by giving an account "of

why it happened," which usually means connecting it to an earlier event as the cause, "together with some account of the causal mechanism connecting the two events" (1989, 3). Elster thus employs exactly the approach to explanation that is characteristic of the scientific realist metaphysic.

The very virtues that allowed rational-choice theory to stand proudly under the positivistic aegis (and to stand almost alone, at least in political science) were its reliance on universal laws (all persons are self-interested) and its rigorous logical deduction from these universals to testable predictions about behavior. Elster jettisons these techniques: General laws, he says, are not effective in explanation because they might reflect only superficial correlations (6); one cannot generalize about self-interest, for some actions are clearly altruistic (52–60); adaptation models, which center on causal processes, are preferable to economic models because research finds no evidence of maximization (79). In respect to Hempel and the Received View, Elster remarks only that the view has some weaknesses; yet he does not explicitly dissociate himself from it, nor explicitly adopt the alternative metaphysic that can now be seen to be appropriate.

One finds a similar attitude among scholars such as Moe (1980), Ostrom (1991), and others of the 'new institutionalist' schools: They define themselves as adherents of rational-choice theory, yet find that theory in need of 'minor' modifications. Moe expands the nature of interests that motivate human action to include 'solidary' incentives and 'purposive' incentives, but by so doing he leaves behind the 'universal law' on which rational-choice theory rests. In the same spirit, Ostrom makes a compelling case for the inclusion of political institutions in the study of human societies, but institutions are not universal, they are by their very nature particular. These minor modifications are therefore not at all minor. They create theories that do not fit under the framework of positivism, and they confuse one scientific metaphysic with another. If the classification system is between positivistic science on the one hand, and on the other hand something that is neither positivisitic nor scientific, then the changes in rational-choice theory must be seen as a corruption of a fine theory by the loosening of its rigor. But as the philosophers of science now teach, this dilemma is out of date. And the modifications urged by various political scientists show that scientific realism has been discovered in practice, if not by name.

References

Baer, Michael A., Malcolm E. Jewell, and Lee Sigelman, eds. 1991. *Political Science in America: Oral Histories of a Discipline.* Lexington: University Press of Kentucky.

Ball, Terence, ed. 1987. *Idioms of Inquiry: Critique and Renewal in Political Science.* Albany, NY: SUNY Press.

———. 1987. "Is There Progress in Political Science." In Ball 1987, pp. 13–43.

Bhaskar, Roy. 1975. *A Realist Theory of Science.* Leeds: Leeds Books.

Blalock, Hubert H. Jr. 1984. *Basic Dilemmas in the Social Sciences.* Beverly Hills, CA: Sage Publications.

Bloor, David. [1961] 1976. *Knowledge and Social Imagery.* London: Routledge Kegan Paul.

Brown, S. C., ed. 1979. *Philosophical Disputes in the Social Sciences.* Sussex: Harvester Press.

Campbell, Angus, Philip E. Converse, Warren E. Miller, and Donald E. Stokes. [1960] 1964. *The American Voter.* New York: John Wiley and Sons.

Churchland, Paul M. 1979. *Scientific Realism and the Plasticity of Mind.* Cambridge: Cambridge University Press.

Churchland, Paul M., and Clifford A. Hooker, eds. 1985. *Images of Science: Essays on Realism and Empiricism with a Reply from Bas C. Van Fraassen.* Chicago: University of Chicago Press.

D'Andrade, Roy. 1986. "Three Scientific World Views and the Covering Law Model." In Fiske and Shweder 1986, pp. 19–41.

Donagan, Alan. 1964. "Historical Explanation: The Popper-Hempel Theory Reconsidered." *History and Theory* 6:3–26.

Downs, Anthony. 1957. *An Economic Theory of Democracy.* New York: Harper and Row.

Easton, David. 1990. *The Analysis of Political Structure.* New York: Routledge.

Eckstein, Harry. 1975. "Case Study and Theory in Political Science." In *Handbook of Political Science,* ed. Fred Greenstein and Nelson Polsby, vol. 7, pp. 79–137. Reading, MA: Addison-Wesley.

Ellis, Brian. 1985. "What Science Aims to Do." In Churchland and Hooker 1985, pp. 48–74.

Elster, Jon. 1989. *Nuts and Bolts for the Social Sciences.* Cambridge: Cambridge University Press.

Eulau, Heinz. 1986. *Politics, Self, and Society: A Theme and Variations.* Cambridge: Harvard University Press.

Farr, James. 1987. "Resituating Explanation." In Ball 1987, pp. 45–66.

Feyerabend, Paul. 1975. *Against Method.* Atlantic Highlands, NJ: Humanities Press.

Fiske, Donald W., and Richard A. Shweder, eds. 1986. *Metatheory in Social Science: Pluralisms and Subjectivities.* Chicago: University of Chicago Press.

Friedman, Michael. 1988. "Explanation and Scientific Understanding." In Pitt 1988, pp. 188–98.

Giere, Ronald N. 1985. "Constructive Realism." In Churchland and Hooker 1985, pp. 75–98.

———. 1988. *Explaining Science: A Cognitive Approach.* Chicago: University of Chicago Press.

Glymour, Clark. 1985. "Explanation and Realism." In Churchland and Hooker 1985, pp. 99–117.

Gunnell, John G. 1986. *Between Philosophy and Politics: The Alienation of Political Theory.* Amherst: University of Massachusetts Press.

Hacking, Ian. 1985. "Do We See Through a Microscope?" In Churchland and Hooker 1985, pp. 132–52.

Hardin, Russell. 1987. "Rational Choice Theories." In Ball 1987, pp. 67–91.

Harre, Romano. 1986. *Varieties of Realism: A Rationale for the Natural Sciences.* New York: Basil Blackwell.

———. 1988. "Modes of Explanation." In Hilton 1988, pp. 129–44.

Hempel, Carl Gustav. 1965. *Aspects of Scientific Explanation and Other Essays in the Philosophy of Science.* New York: The Free Press.

Hempel, Carl G., and Paul Oppenhein. [1948] 1988. "Studies in the Logic of

Explanation." In Pitt 1988, pp. 9–50. Originally published in *Philosophy of Science* 15 (1948): 567–79.

Hilton, Denis J., ed. 1988. *Contemporary Science and Natural Explanation: Commonsense Conceptions of Causality.* New York: New York University Press.

Hooker, Clifford A. "Surface Dazzle, Ghostly Depths: An Exposition and Critical Evaluation of Van Fraassen's Vindication of Empiricism Against Realism." In Churchland and Hooker 1985, 153–96.

Hull, David L. 1988. *Science as a Process: An Evolutionary Account of the Social and Conceptual Development of Science.* Chicago: University of Chicago Press.

Isaac, Jeffrey C. 1987. "After Empiricism: The Realistic Alternative." In Ball 1987, pp. 187–205.

Jessor, Richard, ed. 1991. *Perspectives on Behavioral Science: The Colorado Lectures.* Boulder, CO: Westview Press.

King, Gary, Robert O. Keohane, and Sidney Verba. 1994. *Designing Social Inquiry: Scientific Inference in Qualitative Research.* Princeton, NJ: Princeton University Press.

Kitcher, Philip. 1988. "Explanatory Unification." In Pitt 1988, pp. 167–87.

Kuhn, Thomas S. 1962. *The Structure of Scientific Revolutions.* Chicago: University of Chicago Press.

Lakatos, Imre. 1970. "Falsification and the Methodology of Scientific Research Programmes." In Lakatos and Musgrave 1970, pp. 91–196.

Lakatos, Imre, and Alan Musgrave. 1970. *Criticism and the Growth of Knowledge.* London: Cambridge University Press.

Laudan, Larry. 1977. *Progress and Its Problems.* Berkeley: University of California Press.

Lindblom, Charles E. 1990. *Inquiry and Change: The Troubled Attempt to Understand and Shape Society.* New Haven, CT: Yale University Press.

Lindblom, Charles E., and David K. Cohen. 1979. *Usable Knowledge: Social Sciences and Social Problem Solving.* New Haven, CT: Yale University Press.

Lowi, Theodore J. 1992. "The State in Political Science: How We Became What We Study." *American Political Science Review* 86, no. 1 (March): 1–7.

Mannheim, Karl. n.d. *Ideology and Utopia.* New York: Harvest. Originally published in the United States in 1936.

Merton, Robert K. [1949] 1957. *Social Theory and Social Structure.* New York: The Free Press.

Miller, David, ed. 1983. *A Pocket Popper.* Fontana.

Moe, Terry M. 1987. "Interests, Institutions, and Positive Theory: The Politics of the NLRB." In *Studies of American Political Development,* ed. Karen Orren and Stephen Skowronek, vol. 2, pp. 236–99.

Moon, J. Donald. 1975. "The Logic of Political Inquiry: A Synthesis of Opposed Perspectives." In *Handbook of Political Science,* ed. Fred Greenstein and Nelson Polsby, pp. 131–228. Reading, MA: Addison-Wesley.

Musgrave, Alan. 1985. "Realism Versus Constructive Empiricism." In Churchland and Hooker 1985, pp. 197–221.

Nelson, John S. 1975. "Accidents, Laws, and Philosophic Flaws." *Comparative Politics* 7 (April): 435–57.

Ostrom, Elinor. 1991. "Rational Choice Theory and Institutional Analysis: Toward Complementarity." *American Political Science Review* 85, no. 1 (March): 237–43.

Pitt, Joseph C., ed. 1988. *Theories of Explanation.* New York: Oxford University Press.

Popper, Karl R. 1972. *Objective Knowledge: An Evolutionary Approach.* London: Oxford University Press.

———. 1990. "Political Science and the Crisis of Authoritarianism." *American Political Science Review* 84, no. 1 (March): 3–19.

Pye, Lucian W. 1968. "Description, Analysis, and Sensitivity to Change." In *Political Science and Public Policy,* ed. Austin Ranney, pp. 239–61. Chicago: Markham.

Railton, Peter. 1988. "A Deductive-nomological Model of Probabilistic Explanation." In Pitt 1988, pp. 118–35.

Ricci, David M. 1984. *The Tragedy of Political Science: Scholarship and Democracy.* New Haven, CT: Yale University Press.

Riker, William H. 1962. *The Theory of Political Coalitions.* New Haven, CT: Yale University Press.

Roelofs, H. Mark. 1994. "Two Ways to Political Science: Critical and Descriptive." *PS: Political Science and Politics* 27, no. 2 (June): 264–68.

Root, Michael. 1993. *Philosophy of Social Science: Methods, Ideals and Politics of Social Inquiry.* Oxford: Blackwell.

Sayer, Andrew. 1992. *Method in Social Science: A Realistic Approach.* London: Routledge.

Scriven, Michael. 1988. "Explanations, Predictions, and Laws." In Pitt 1988, pp. 51–74.

Secord, Paul F. 1986. "Explanation in the Social Sciences and in Life Situations." In *Metatheory in Social Science: Pluralisms and Subjectivities,* ed. Donald W. Fiske and Richard A. Shweder, pp. 197–221. Chicago: University of Chicago Press.

Seidelman, Raymond, with Edward J. Harpham. 1985. *Disenchanted Realists: Political Science and the American Crisis 1884–1984.* Albany, NY: SUNY Press. With a rejoinder by Skocpol, pp. 86–96.

Shapin, Steven. 1982. "History of Science and its Sociolocal Reconstructions." *History of Science* 20 (September): 157–211.

Simkin, Colin. 1993. *Popper's Views on Natural and Social Science.* Leiden: Brill.

Somit, Albert, and Joseph Tanenhaus. 1967. *The Development of Political Science: From Burgess to Behavioralism.* Boston: Allyn and Bacon.

Stinchcombe, Arthur L. 1968. *Constructing Social Theories.* New York: Harcourt, Brace, World.

Stouffer, Samuel A. 1965. *Communism, Conformity, and Civil Liberties.* Gloucester: Peter Smith.

Suppe, Frederick. 1989. *The Semantic Conception of Theories and Scientific Realism.* Urbana and Chicago: University of Illinois Press.

Sylvan, David, and Barry Glassner. 1985. *A Rationalist Methodology for the Social Sciences.* New York: Basil Blackwell.

Turnbull, William, and Ben Slugowski. 1988. "Conversational and Linguistic Processes in Causal Attribution." In Hilton 1988, pp. 66–93.

Van Fraassen, Bas C. 1980. *The Scientific Image*. Oxford: Oxford University Press.

Wendt, Alexander, and Ian Shapiro. 1993. "The Misunderstood Promise of 'Realist Social Theory.' " Paper presented at the annual meeting of the American Political Science Association. Washington, DC: September.

Wildavsky, Aaron. 1987. "Choosing Preferences by Constructing Institutions: A Cultural Theory of Preference Formation." *American Political Science Review* 81, no. 1 (March): 3–21.

Winch, Peter. 1958. *The Idea of a Social Science*. London: Routledge Kegan Paul.

Index

Ruth Lane teaches political research methods and comparative politics in the Department of Government, School of Public Affairs, American University. Her research interests include cognitive science, research-oriented theory, and computer modeling.

9 781563 249402